Minding the Whole Person

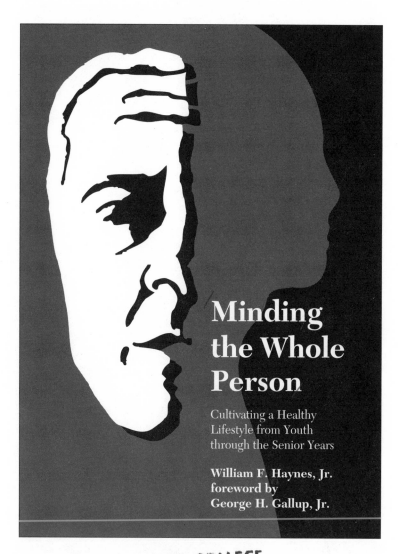

Minding the Whole Person

Cultivating a Healthy
Lifestyle from Youth
through the Senior Years

William F. Haynes, Jr.
foreword by
George H. Gallup, Jr.

A Campion Book

Loyola University Press
Chicago

Loyola University Press
3441 North Ashland Avenue
Chicago, Illinois 60657

Cover and interior design by Nancy Gruenke

Library of Congress Cataloging-in-Publication Data
Haynes, William F.,
    Minding the whole person: cultivating a healthy lifestyle from youth
through the senior years / by William Haynes F.
        p.   cm.
    Includes bibliographical references and index.
    ISBN 0-8294-0778-2
    1. Aged–Health and hygiene. 2. Aged–Diseases. 3. Aging.
I. Title
    [DNLM: 1. Mental Healing. 2. Aging–psychology. 3. Religion and
Medicine   WB 880 H424m 1994]
RA777.6.H38   1994
613'.0438–dc20
DNLM / DLC   94-12238
for Library of Congress   CIP

This year and every year, appreciation for:
the beautifully constructed body temple,
the kingdom of God within,
God's ever-present grace,
—unearned gifts,
yet available to all.

Contents

Foreword

F or the first time in history a majority of Americans are dying not from unconquered diseases, but from self-inflicted problems, such as smoking, alcohol abuse, lack of exercise, use of illegal drugs, and poor diet.

Why do Americans appear to be submitting to such self-destructive tendencies? The root cause may be spiritual malaise—feelings of emptiness and disconnectedness from God and one's fellow human beings, even a sense of hopelessness about the state of the nation and the world.

One result of such bleak feelings can be the heedless pursuit of pleasure, living for the moment and for oneself and failing to take time off from the fast pace of life for reflection and the reordering of one's life.

Happily, surveys document two countertrends that may in the long run be profoundly healing both for individuals and for society: namely, a search for spiritual moorings and meaning in life and, related to this, a search for deeper and more meaningful relationships with other people. Quite often this search takes the form of small groups where deep hurts and needs can be shared and healed.

Now comes an important book for our times. *Minding the Whole Person* speaks directly and powerfully to the spiritual needs of the populace and its desire to experience wholeness. The central problem of this age, writes Dr. William Haynes, is that people today are trying to maintain control of their own lives instead of submitting to the power of the Lord and discovering that when we surrender to the Lord's wishes we find our real selves and our real purpose in life.

The author describes the whole person as a three-legged stool—mind, spirit, and body—noting that if one leg is missing the stool will not function. He writes: "It behooves all of us to make the most of our unique gifts and to use them to constantly keep the body temple at its highest level of efficiency so to better serve God, our fellows, and ourselves."

Dr. Haynes discusses a wide range of health matters, including cardiovascular disease, exercise, depression, and nutrition and also takes a look into the future, examining the difficult ethical issues of organ transplants and genetic engineering.

This is a solid book that can stand alone for its wealth of vital information on the latest discoveries in the field of health and medicine and how these discoveries relate to the aging process in the social context of the United States today. It is, however, much more. *Minding the Whole Person* is not only a manual for good health it is also a guide to a full and meaningful life.

A strong message of faith shines forth from the author's works—faith forged by life experiences, by his work as a doctor, and by his commitment to deepening his relationship with the Lord. Dr. Haynes is not a detached observer or bystander—he is actively interested in the psychological and spiritual well-being of his patients. He prays with those in his care, noting that this element of spirituality "adds a new aspect to the professional relationship." It is, he believes, "a unique opportunity that will change [the physician's] whole approach to medicine."

The author's God is not a distant God, but a God who is actively interested in the details of our lives, who listens, heals, and works with and through us, if we in humble obedience are willing to listen. The spirituality of which Dr. Haynes writes is not a vague, free-floating kind of spirituality, but one rooted in history and in God's reconciling love for humankind, made known in the life and death of Jesus Christ. By quoting appropriate scripture passages throughout the book, Dr. Haynes never lets the reader forget the biblical basis of his message.

Dr. Haynes is well qualified to bring his book and its important message to the public. A practicing internist and cardiologist for over thirty years, Dr. Haynes practices what he prescribes. He is a conscientious doctor who keeps on top of health trends, even outside his own specialty. He has an active faith life, devoting part of each morning to prayer, meditation, and scripture reading. He has even been known to make house calls to pray for a patient's recovery. On one of his days off last fall Dr. Haynes came to my home to pray with me when I was in a deeply worried state following an operation for cancer. I can attest to the fact that when a believing doctor prays for you it touches something very deep within your soul. The author rejoices in recoveries and never fails to thank God.

As for the third part of the body temple—the body itself—Dr. Haynes follows a regular regime of swimming (he is a Masters swimmer) and other forms of exercise.

Older readers will gain encouragement from *Minding the Whole Person,* both from its practical advice as well as its reminders that we can, with God's grace, grow old gracefully and healthfully. But young readers will profit as well as they struggle to unite their minds, spirits, and bodies into the whole and integrated persons God intends them to be. It is fervently hoped that young people heed the messages in this book because the nation is facing an unprecedented adolescent health crisis. Studies reveal that, for the first time in the history of this country, young people are less healthy and less prepared to take their places in society than were their parents.

For many years Dr. Haynes has healed in the name of Christ through his hands and through prayer. Now with *Minding the Whole Person* his healing ministry can take another great leap forward.

One of the author's favorite meditations is from the Book of Isaiah (50:4–5).

> The Lord GOD has given me
>   a well-trained tongue,
> That I might know how to speak to
>   the weary
>   a word that will rouse them.
> Morning after morning
>   he opens my ear that I may hear;
> And I have not rebelled,
>   have not turned back.

This passage is one that clearly sustains Dr. Haynes in his life and work and points to those personal qualities that give his mission and message such power for today's world: that of teacher, healer, and obedient servant of God.

George H. Gallup, Jr.
Chairman, George H. Gallup International Institute
Princeton, New Jersey

Introduction

L ike most of us you have been living a busy life, raising a family, working hard and have barely noticed the rapidly passing years. You wake up suddenly one morning with the shocking revelation that you are in your fifth or sixth decade of life! "No, it can't be true!" you say to yourself. "Where has the time gone?" A myriad of events, not necessarily important or connected and spanning some forty or fifty years, flash through your mind. The astounding realization that you are getting older and that you may even die one day brings with it the uncomfortable feeling that you have been transformed overnight into a "senior citizen." Before long you might even be "elderly." And so you begin to evaluate your aging faculties, starting with the clarity of your thinking processes. With some relief you realize that you seem to be correctly aware of time, place, and person. At least you've got one thing going for you. You now examine your physical side, and you note that all four extremities appear to be working and intact and breathing seems normal. Sensing your own mortality, perhaps for the first time, you then begin to consider your spiritual compo-nent. Do you have a good relationship with God, and how close are you to acknowledging his presence in all things? These are heavy issues!

Having been a practicing internist and cardiologist for over thirty years, I have found two things to be clear. First, we are all definitely getting older—all of us with no exceptions.

Second, each of us is an integration of three components: the emotional, the physical, and the spiritual. All three are equally important and necessary and compose what may be termed the *body temple*. Should one part be missing or greatly diminished, the body will malfunction. In my particular vocation I deal daily with patients who suffer from some degree of brokenness—be it psychological, physical, spiritual, or all three. There are endless combinations of malfunctioning parts. A delicate interconnection exists between the mind, the body, and the spirit in virtually all cases of illness as well as wellness. This relationship has led me to an increasing interest in the effect of aging upon the body temple and in how well a given individual weathers life's many storms. The question I ask myself and others is, How well has the occupant treated his or her temple? Is it receiving the love and respect that this special gift deserves? As I focus more closely on the body temple, other questions automatically follow. Is the body being used to its fullest capacity (we must "use the body" by exercising or "lose the body" to poor health)? What can we do to prevent premature decline or damage? How can we make the body temple function at its best? What is the relationship between the physical cure of a medical condition and an inner healing? The physician may help the body recover from pneumonia, or the psychiatrist may explain the reason for a certain behavior pattern, but neither provide inner healing. Why? you might ask. Inner healing and inner peace are gifts of God's grace. A question of paramount importance therefore is, Just what is the role of daily prayer in attaining and maintaining our wholeness? If prayer is a vital link to healing, are we open to it? Other factors such as stress have an impact upon the body temple as we age. Have we received the gift of inner peace that God so anxiously wants to give us?

Since the body is aging and is subject to accidents and illness, some parts of the body may need replacement. Can they be replaced? If so, which ones? What hope is there for the body in the future, that is, what can we hope for in genetic engineering and creative medical and surgical research? Finally, how can we help others by donating parts of our body temple through organ transplantations? Despite the many technological advances in these areas, we still must rely upon God's presence for the strength and faith to go on living in the knowledge of his love and trusting in his perfect plan for each of us. But because of the frantic pace of life, we often don't put aside the time to listen to God to know him better and to allow ourselves to be transformed by him. It is through the discipline of daily prayer, and through constant awareness of his presence, that we will become more Christ-like. We must not ignore the kingdom of God within while relying on human-kind's biotechnological advances, as wonderful as they may be. It stands, therefore, that the healthy individual must blend all three elements (mind, body, and spirit), into a well-integrated whole to function at the highest level every day.

The central part and core of our body temple is the Spirit of God within. We may be physically beautiful and psychologi-cally healthy, but it is the spirit of God within that is our source of strength, joy, and peace; it is the lighthouse of the body temple. Each of us are children of God; each of us has special gifts and is loved just the way we are. By living in the spirit, we learn to praise God for the good and bad in our lives. Even the "bad things" that happen may be God's way of leading us back to him, may be an opportunity for spiritual growth and for opening ourselves to his guidance. When we are better able to attain wholeness, we are better able to reach out to others. A spiritually broken body temple cannot be an effective channel of healing for others. By loving God with our whole self and by being loved by him, we can love our neighbors—neighbors from all races and cultures—as we love ourselves.

> So then you are no longer strangers and aliens, but you are citizens with the saints and also members of the household of God, built upon the foundation of the apos-tles and the prophets, with Christ Jesus himself the cornerstone. In him the whole structure is joined together and grows into a holy temple in the Lord; in whom you also are built together spiritually into a dwelling place of God.
>
> –Ephesians 2:19–22

In a similar manner, the very ill patient must be cared for by taking into consideration the impact the illness has upon the body as a whole. Treatment directed only to one component of the temple will be less effective than treatment directed to all three components as a unit. For this reason the power of prayer should not be ignored when treating the whole person. Recent research has strongly suggested a connection between peace of mind and enhanced healing and an improved immune system.

French physician Jacques Sarano so aptly expressed these sentiments in 1966:

> If physicians have too much neglected the importance of the spiritual life of their patients and the enormous role that it plays in their health, the philosophers and theologians for their part, have too much neglected the importance of the body. A double movement is therefore necessary, a reciprocal discovery, a dialogue, a breach in the party wall.[1]

The aging process waits for no one, and as we arrive in the mid to later years of our lives, we may become aware of our own finiteness. Philosophical questions that we may have suppressed or not faced when we were younger now come into sharper focus. Questions such as, What have I done with my life? Have I accomplished as much as I had hoped to do? Have I accepted the fact that I may never attain my highest expectations? Have I experienced the joy of God's presence in the past as well as the present? Do I carry with me the inner peace of knowing that God has a perfect plan for me? Do I set aside a quiet time every day to better ascertain what this plan is? Do I see his hand in all that happens in my life and am I therefore able to let him lead me, or must I have complete control? In other words, Do I really trust the Lord, or do I place my "self" in command?

> The Lord will guide you continually,
> and satisfy your needs in parched places,
> and make your bones strong;
> and you shall be like a watered garden,
> like a spring of water,
> whose waters never fail.
> –Isaiah 58:11

Are we really listening? Do we hear what God is trying to tell us?

> I will instruct you and teach you the way you should go;
> I will counsel you with my eye upon you.
>   –Psalm 32:8

Losing absolute control of our lives is a very tall order for many, especially today in the era of "independent" people. The thought of being guided by the Lord rather than the self can be both unreal and frightening. This concept is well illustrated by Paul Pierson.

> Taking the yoke of Christ upon us means making a commitment that requires us to unlearn the human concept of "being on our own." When we do, we attain a conscious awareness of the Christ presence that is always attending us and ready to work through us. We lose our sense of ego. When we grow into a true awareness of oneness with the Christ presence, we have taken on the spirit of Christ as well.[2]

Henri Nouwen, in his book *Show Me the Way,* clarifies the interrelationship of the ego and God this way: "However as soon as I say, 'God exists,' my existence no longer can remain in the center, because the essence of the knowledge of God reveals my own existence as deriving its total being from his." He goes on to say, "The converted person sees, hears and understands with a divine eye, a divine ear, a divine heart."[3]

But, what is happening to the other parts of the body temple? Has my physical body been totally neglected and suffering from years of abuse caused by an unhealthy lifestyle? Am I an emotional wreck? Is my life a daily thunderstorm? Is burnout just around the corner? Or am I aware of the necessity of integrating my mind, body, and spirit in order to function at the highest level for myself as well as to better serve the common good?

What can I do to heal the body temple at this point? I know that the body continues to age, so what lifestyle choices are still open to me? What advances in medicine, surgery, and genetic engineering are likely to be helpful in the future? Most of all, where does prevention of disease play a role? Is it too late for me to change where change is warranted?

The following, from Haggai 1:4–7, is so pertinent that it could have been written today:

> Is it a time for you yourselves to live in your paneled houses, while this house lies in ruins? Now therefore thus says the Lord of hosts: Consider how you have fared. You have sown much, and harvested little; you eat, but you never have enough; you drink, but you never have your fill; you clothe yourselves, but no one is warm; and you that earn wages earn wages to put them into a bag with holes. Thus says the Lord of hosts: Consider how you have fared.

In this book I will first define the meaning and composition of the body temple from the viewpoints of both ancient and modern theologians and philosophers. Then I will discuss the parts of the temple that may change and degenerate with the aging process. I believe that some of these "normal changes," that is, physiological and biochemical changes, which appear to be out of our control, in reality are greatly influenced by our health habits. I will also examine what society has called "normal aging." For example, elderly people are generally expected to be unsteady on their feet and doze in a chair all day, but such degeneration is not necessarily imminent. Many other misconceptions about aging will also be discussed. I will examine the aging process in general as well as the aging heart and coronary arteries. Other bodily systems will be addressed briefly with regard to the aging process: decreased flexibility, hearing loss, balance problems, and insomnia. Additional items associated with aging that I will discuss include osteoporosis, poor nutrition, depression, Alzheimer's disease, and forgetfulness. Stress after retirement and the inevitable social, economical, political, and medical implications for and challenges to older people will also be explored. The concept of aerobic exercise as the "fountain of youth" and the avoidance of tobacco and drug abuse as prerequisites to keeping the body temple out of trouble will be considered. Finally, I will examine a few of the newer medical and surgical advances on the horizon. It behooves all of us to make the most of our unique gifts and to use them to constantly keep the body temple at its highest possible level of efficiency so to better serve God, our fellows, and ourselves. In view of that, the question remains, What is my state of wholeness?

This book will help readers reflect upon some of these issues. Actual cases will illustrate how some of my patients first reacted to these questions, what they did to correct malfunction, and how this not only added to their own quality of life and wholeness but even served as an inspiration to others. The cases will touch upon all age groups—struggling human beings like you and me. In order to preserve confidentiality, the names and some of the backgrounds of the patients have been altered. Suggestions for further reading accompany most chapters.

Further Reading

Daily Word (Unity School of Christianity, Unity Village, Mo.).

This little monthly pamphlet is an old friend, a source of hope, consolation, and courage for over fifty years. I use this along with other reading material every morning during my "quiet time." Its main strength is one of affirming prayer, that is, thanking God for taking over my life, for his perfect plan, and for enhancing my ability to trust in the execution of his plan. God's plan applies to all relationships and situations he places in our path.

Jacques Sarano, *The Meaning of the Body*, trans. by James H. Farley (Philadelphia: Westminster Press, 1966).

This is a good reference for bringing out the vital link between the spiritual and the physical nature of humanity. Dr. Sarano urges us to revere our body, to look after it and cherish it, and to see it as a gift from God.

1

A Christian Physician's View of the Body Temple

Or do you not know that your body is a temple of the Holy Spirit within you, which you have from God, and that you are not your own? For you were bought with a price; therefore glorify God in your body.

–1 Corinthians 6:19–20

God's goal for humankind is for us to draw closer to him as we age. Our bodies locate us in time and place. As God is love, our bodies are necessary to communicate our love to other humans. It is necessary to be in relationships with others in order to progress in our spiritual journey. We love and appreciate God and his love for us, but we also need to love and to be loved by other human beings. We inhabit our own bodies, but we also inhabit a greater body—a body of believers, a community of worshipers, all children of God, regardless of religious tradition.

For just as the body is one and has many members, and all the members of the body, though many, are one body, so it is with Christ. For in the one Spirit we were all baptized into one body—Jews or Greeks, slaves or free—and we were all made to drink of one Spirit. Indeed, the body does not consist of one member but of many.

–1 Corinthians 12:12–14

From a Christian perspective, one belongs to the Body of Christ. This being the case, the manner in which we individually manage our own body temple has not only personal ramifications, but influences the body of Christ—the family of believers—as well. Paul goes on to say:

> As it is, there are many members, yet one body. . . . If one member suffers, all suffer together with it; if one member is honored, all rejoice together with it.
> —1 Corinthians 12:20, 26

As written in *The Word among Us,* a daily missal, "The life of Jesus in us does not remain just a personal and interior thing; it wells up within us and must be expressed to others."[1] As Christians, we are in Christ, and he is in us. Since God is in all, we are one with all God's creatures and all creation, and they are one with us. God wants all of us in the world to be one; a unified "body" with God. This is possible only because all of us are reconciled to him, a forgiveness of sins granted to us by Jesus' death on the cross.

We sometimes forget that our lifestyle, for better or worse, has an impact on those around us, especially those close to us or those connected by family, religious, or other community ties. We cannot live a life in isolation; we are all connected in some form or another, and how we treat our own body reflects on the other members of the body of Christ.

Murray Bodo, O.F.M., in his book *The Way of St. Francis,* states the following:

> A conversion is a turning around, a change of heart; and mortification is the process of saying good-bye to what is not of God, to what is preventing us from experiencing true peace and joy. The modern mortification is to start taking care of our health once more out of reverence for who we are: temples of the Spirit of God.[2]

Bodo believes that we have a responsibility to take care of our bodies, which includes being alert to the potentially harmful effects of alcohol, drugs, tobacco, and chemicals.

Barbara Shlemon is a Christian therapist interested in retreats devoted to inner healing. She states:

The only way we can keep the love of Jesus is to give it away to others. Discovering ways to relieve the sufferings of those around us can bring many blessings into our life, keeping us firmly planted in the Lord's will.[3]

In other words, when the temple is destroyed, there is a need for inner healing as well as physical or outer healing. As Bodo goes on to say,

True religion is loving God with my whole soul and my whole mind and my whole body as a whole person. It is only when I am one that I can love others properly, because I love them as myself. If my self is divided, so will be my love of others.[4]

People have been interested in the interconnection between mind and body since biblical days. Genesis 2 clearly depicts human beings as a combination of the psychological and the physical. James discusses the interconnection of body and spirit, but outreach to others, a component so vital to the Christian, is always in the background.

For just as the body without the spirit is dead, so faith without works is also dead.

–James 2:26

Early in his vocation, Augustine of Hippo, A.D. 354–430, considered the body a snare for evil and believed that bodily pleasures should be avoided. He felt that one's energies should be focused away from the body and toward higher philosophical and intellectual concerns. This belief degraded the body and compartmentalized the body temple. However, in the later part of his life, he changed his opinion about the body and its sensory parts. He wrote:

If through the flesh, Christ hath greatly profited us, how does the flesh profit us nothing? But it is through the flesh that the spirit acted for our salvation. . . . For how should the sound of the Word reach us except through the voice of the flesh?[5]

He carried his belief in the mind-body connection further by advocating that well-founded cases of miraculous healings should be recorded:

> I have been concerned that such accounts should be published because I saw that signs of divine power like those of older days were frequently in modern times too, and I felt that they should not pass into oblivion, unnoticed by people in general.[6]

In his book *Body Theology,* theologian Arthur A. Vogel notes, "The Christian God, who wanted human beings to know him as a person became incarnate—took a body—for that very reason."[7] He goes on to say that human beings are more than bodily locations and must reach out beyond themselves. He adds, "Experiencing the presence of other people is the only key we have for recognizing the presence of God; God present to us in and through their presence."[8]

In other words, as Charles Davis, another theologian, wrote:

> To accept the human body, or better, the bodily reality and presence of human persons, is to respond positively to bodies as humanly expressive even when they do not have perfect physical form. . . .

> The bodily beauty of men and women, the beauty that shines forth physically, is not purely physical. Facial beauty, insofar as it comes from perfect physical proportions, firm flesh, and finely textured skin, can of itself be dead and unattractive.[9]

The Lord said to Samuel,

> Do not look on his appearance or on the height of his stature, because I have rejected him; for the Lord does not see as mortals see; they look on the outward appearance, but the Lord looks on the heart.
>
> —1 Samuel 16:7

What Is Meant by the "Body Temple"?

Our body, its glories and its miseries, its sicknesses and its thousand deaths, is the language that we speak to God and to men; but it is also the language that God addresses to us through our humility. Our body is his message.[10]

In the practice of medicine, there is a growing interest in spirituality as it relates to patient care. A greater awareness of the inner core of the individual, the quiet place where one speaks to God and he speaks to us, is developing. Theologian Martin Marty, in a study published in the *New York Times,* finds it "astonishing that in a high-tech, highly affluent nation, we have 90 percent who identify themselves as religious."[11] This opinion poll, which surveyed 113,000 people in the U.S., is thought to be the largest survey on religious affiliation to date. The spiritual component of the body temple plays a potentially enormous role in dealing with patients. It is the key to our wholeness. "Every decision we make will be guided by the Christ mind, which is the perfect mind of God in us. We seek wisdom from within—listen for instruction from that true, inner voice."[12] The physical body may be thought of as the covering for our mind and spirit. When the spirit and mind die, so does the physical component. But when the physical part dies, the spirit lives on into eternity; we all trust that this will be so in heaven.

Many athletes with excellent bodies and good minds recognize the importance of the spiritual side of their being. A 1991 article in the *New York Times* noted that some professional athletes expressed their support of religion by donating 10 percent of their income to furthering God's work. The article went on to mention that as many as 40 percent of all major league baseball players participate in Baseball Chapel (an athletic, religious organization), league-wide in scope, which is also associated with bible study groups.[13] There is no doubt that many professional athletes with large salaries and multiple benefits may still feel that something is missing from their lives. Inner peace is the gem that no amount of fame or material goods can buy. It is the priceless gift of the Holy Spirit. Giving of oneself as well as of one's material goods to those in need (such as tithing to one's church or religious organization) is a way of receiving this gift of inner peace. Many give of themselves by inspiring and encouraging teenagers. Relief pitcher for the New York Yankees Lee Guetterman was quoted, "I make $1 million a year, and I give 10 percent to my church." He went on to say, "Then I set aside another 5 percent for other things. When I give that away, I tell myself, 'That's it. You've given 15 percent.'" Other baseball players who have donated a portion of their income to religious organizations include Darryl Strawberry, Glen Davis, Orel Hershiser, Howard Johnson, Kevin Maas, Gary Carter, Tim Burke, and Tony Gwynn. Football players Reggie White and Barry Sanders as well as golfers Scott Simpson and Billy Casper make similar donations. Many athletes are now more open to thank God for all of their blessings and athletic success and are not afraid to share this with television audiences. For example, it is no longer rare to see a football player, upon making a touchdown, cross himself while kneeling in the end zone or to see several basketball teammates kneel down to pray before the start of a game. They recognize that it is by God's grace that they have been given their excellent physique and talents; and they are willing to acknowledge this in public.

In my life, over the past ten years, I have yearned for and been drawn to our heavenly Father. I have felt beckoned to be part of God in all I do and to have him part of me. This feeling began a decade ago when I was going through a serious personal crisis in my life. Sometimes God uses a crisis to awaken us if we have not been listening to him, especially if we have been too "busy" doing other things. Since that time I have read over 300 books devoted to inner healing and the power of the Holy Spirit and have attended about a dozen retreats on inner healing. I had an unquenchable thirst for God's presence.

> As a deer longs for flowing streams, so my soul longs for you, O God.
> My soul thirsts for God, for the living God.
> When shall I come and behold the face of God?
> —Psalm 42:1–2

William A. Barry, S.J., describes this overwhelming drawing of our hearts to God:

The deepest desire of our hearts is for God. While we are in the throes of this desire, everything else we might desire takes a back seat, as it were. Everything else becomes relative before the absolute Mystery we desire. Moreover, insofar as this desire reigns in our hearts, we also desire to live out our lives in harmony with this desire.[14]

My own brokenness was necessary for God to firmly grasp me and make me his own—to make me humble and forcibly open me to his unlimited love and grace.

However, I also needed to give attention to the emotional and physical aspects of my body temple. The peace of mind that is so elusive in the secular world of power and materialism can only be truly found through growth toward oneness with our Lord—the process of becoming more Christ-like as we become more aware of his presence within. How many times have we heard the anguishing question, Is this all there is in life?—a question that often comes from someone who has all the material comforts money can buy. It is through prayer and daily quiet times with our Lord that we are able to experience ongoing inner healings and the joy of inner peace. These are God's gifts to us through his grace. We cannot rely on our strength alone as we attempt to be his servants. Murray Bodo states, "Christ alone is the fullness of life, and the compulsive pursuit of money, more than anything else, distracts the individual from what really brings life. And it is what happens at the core of the individual which ultimately determines what society will become."[15] When we reach out to others, we begin to appreciate the beginnings of true happiness. Inner peace, which comes from the core of the individual, begins to replace the drive toward the greater accumulation of excessive material goods.

All who make idols are nothing, and the things they delight in do not profit; their witnesses neither see nor know. And so they will be put to shame.

–Isaiah 44:9

Perhaps the professional athletes mentioned above and many of the rest of us have come to the realization that helping others brings the greatest reward possible—inner peace. No amount of material wealth can replace this priceless commodity.

This inner peace, this gift of God, is a prize unto itself, but, in addition, it has a very important role to play in regulating the responses of our body to the outside world. It influences the autonomic nervous system, hormone secretions, the diurnal body rhythms, the immune system, the healing process, our emotional state, and our physical health. William Johnston, an American Jesuit and mystic interested in the relationship of Zen and prayer to body function and well-being wrote, "There is a basic rhythm in the body, linked to a consciousness that is deeper than is ordinarily experienced. . . . anyone who wants to meditate in depth must find this rhythm and the consciousness that accompanies it." He carries this thought further by saying that Western prayer is often too mind- or brain-oriented and not "with the deeper layers of the body where the power to approach the spiritual is generated."[16] If the spiritual nature of human beings is so important, it is surprising that we physicians have so frequently ignored the spiritual aspect in medical practice. No medical school curriculum to my knowledge contains a course on the spirituality of the patient. Are we afraid to speak of God in a lecture? Are we being trapped by some sort of church-state–separation monster that will devour us if we mention God even though we make no attempt to proselytize? Are we too timid to acknowledge what most people already feel—that there is a supreme being?

Psychotherapists are beginning to view religious beliefs as an aid to mental health. This is quite a turnaround, as many psychologists formerly had described religion as merely an illusion. In a September 1991 article in the *New York Times,* one therapist noted that patients with strong religious ties generally have a more positive view on life, more empathy, and less depression than patients who do not.[17] As Vogel so nicely put it, "Because we are members of the human community by virtue of our bodies—because our bodies have an outside and therefore constantly relate us to others—our bodies are meant to be our ever-present means of expressing God's love for all men."[18] The Christian tradition recognizes that we are not only made up of individual bodies but are members of a larger body, the body of Christ, a community of worshipers that takes part in church services, the eucharist, retreats, bible study groups, and prayer groups.

As a whole the person is regarded much like a three-legged stool; if one leg is missing or broken, the stool will not function. By incorporating this concept into treatment of the human person, I hope to explain how all three aspects are integral parts of the body temple and demonstrate how each part plays a necessary role in maintaining wholeness as we age.

Further Reading

Murray Bodo, O.F.M. *The Way of St. Francis* (New York: Image/Doubleday, 1984).

I've read a good number of books about St. Francis, but this book appeals to me the most. It is well written and makes St. Francis come alive and become part of one's daily life. Bodo weaves Francis's life with Christ's life so that the reader is better able to understand the continued popularity of Francis and the continued growth of the Franciscan movement. Francis serves as a beacon as we, along with him, try to become more Christ-like.

William Johnston, S.J., *Christian Zen* (New York: Harper and Row, 1973).

Christian Zen allows the reader to explore and incorporate the power of centering prayer found in the Eastern church and other eastern religions into one's own daily worship. Frequently during centering prayer one is able to experience "the peace that passeth all understanding" by being quiet in the presence of God. Johnston feels we often are too cerebral in our approach to prayer and may need to dig deeper into our consciousness in order to experience God's presence.

The Word among Us (Box 6003, Gaithersburg, Md. 20897-8403).

This missal is the second item that I read during my early morning "quiet time." It serves as a commentator for the daily mass and relates the day's scripture lessons to today's world.

2

Prayer and Healing

In a sense, physicians stand by while the body heals itself. Modern medicine aids the body by prescribing medicines for disease, determining proper nutrition, and in general providing the best conditions for healing to take place. The healer provides the expertise to interpret the proper diagnostic tests and give the proper treatment as well as compassion, humility, and frequently faith. Audible prayer is also a very effective way to establish optimal healing conditions, if the patient is receptive to it. If there is some doubt about the patient's openness to audible prayer, inaudible prayer or a reassuring touch may act as a silent prayer. Through prayer, a new relationship—a spiritual one—develops between the patient and the physician, especially when audible prayer is used in conjunction with the laying on of hands. But the physician must always be sensitive to the individual's openness to audible prayer.

A dozen years ago I went through a very dark period in my life. At that same time I admitted Barry, a forty-five-year-old freelance writer, to the hospital coronary care unit with a heart attack. He had both the star of David and a cross hung on a chain around his neck. I remember thinking that here was a man who had more than one base covered. After starting all the necessary medical treatments, I sat down at his bedside. Much to my astonishment, he turned to me and asked if he could pray for me! He remarked that he sensed I was carrying a very heavy burden. He was correct, and I readily accepted his prayers. He actually prayed for me daily after that. The strange thing was that, although he was the one suffering from the heart attack, he discerned that I was suffering from a "heavy heart," though physically I seemed well. I was in need of an inner healing. After his hospital discharge, I saw Barry regularly at office visits. He continued to pray for me, brought a number of books on inner healing, and even anointed me with oil. He, in turn, allowed me to pray for him, giving thanks to God for the healing of his heart. The traditional doctor-patient relationship certainly existed between the two of us, but, for the first time in my career, I also had a new connection—a spiritual one—with a patient. As with so many patients since then, this additional spiritual link has been very important and special for me as I try to bring God into the healing process. I wrote about many of my subsequent experiences in *A Physician's Witness to the Power of Shared Prayer* (Loyola University Press 1990). The role of spirituality in patient care must be recognized by physicians as a powerful asset in the healing process. Even should the health-care provider be an agnostic or atheist, he or she should at least appreciate the clergy or hospital chaplain as a valuable resource. But once one has the gift of discernment and senses the patient's receptivity to prayer, what a wonderful blessing it is to act as a channel for God's healing love! In my view, everyone receives a blessing: the patient, the clergy member (if one is present), and the health-care provider. For certain, a new and wonderful relationship is created—one built upon equality as children of God, which adds a new aspect to the professional relationship.

In prayer, physicians have a unique opportunity that will change their whole approach to medicine. For the physician, the joy and caring that emanates from the sharing prayer, when added to the ability to use medical know-how, brings an entirely new perspective to medical practice. Sharing prayer has many other positive effects: patients are often more compliant, that is, they take medications as directed, keep appointments more regularly, and make positive lifestyle changes. I remember a middle-aged man who had recently stopped smoking who said at a follow-up office visit, "I wanted to start smoking again but since you cared enough to pray with me about it, I didn't want to let you down. I'm sure I would have been tempted to start again otherwise."

But I hasten to repeat that the key word in sharing prayer is *discernment*. If the physician senses that the patient is not open to prayer, it is best to let the prayer be a mere touch or to pray inaudibly. Not every patient is open to audible prayer and not every physician is either. The physician may eventually need the experience of a prayer group, a retreat, or personal spiritual direction before attempting prayer with patients. Of course, much of what I say applies to prayer-givers regardless of vocation and is not limited to physicians. Jesus wants us all to be "wounded healers"—the lay person, clergy, or physician, who carries the same hurts as the person to whom he or she is minstering. This empathy enables the healer to pray with authenticity; his or her own suffering is a source of understanding and compassion. Brother Roger, the founder of Taizé, an ecumenical religious community in France, which I was fortunate to visit for a few days in 1988, wrote the following:

> Without forgiveness, there will never be peace. Without compassion, there is no future for human beings. Without forgiveness and reconciliation, there is no future for Christians and the building up of the human family across the earth.[1]

To be evangelists for Christ, we must trust in God and make reconciliation a part of our daily lives.

A San Francisco cardiologist noted therapeutic benefits when employing intercessory prayer for his patients admitted to his hospital's coronary care unit (CCU). His study employed a prospective, randomized double-blind protocol involving 393 patients over a ten-month period. A group of 192 patients permitted a group of Christians to pray for them at a location outside of the hospital. The control group consisted of 201 patients for whom no one prayed (although the subject of prayer was never mentioned during the medical treatment). Both groups were treated the same medically. The results were that the group receiving prayer suffered fewer cases of congestive heart failure, had fewer cardiac arrests, had less need for ventilators (intubation), suffered fewer cases of pneumonia, and had less need for antibiotics and diuretics.[2] At a meeting of the American Psychiatric Association in San Francisco in 1993, Dr. Thomas Oxman, a psychiatrist, presented data showing that there was a fourfold increase in the risk of death within six months following open-heart surgery for patients with no religious beliefs. The study consisted of 212 patients over age fifty-five who were operated upon for elective coronary artery by-pass surgery and/or aortic valve replacement.[3] Many times after praying at the bedside with patients in the CCU I have noted a sigh, a sign of letting go, often followed by weeping as the patient is filled with the Holy Spirit and is released from anxiety. I have also often noted the bedside monitor showing a fall in heart rate as the nervous system begins to calm down. Recent work appears to confirm that a peaceful mind provides a boost to the immune system, while an anxious mind has the opposite effect.

A psychologist's study involving nursing home patients found that listening, touching, and sometimes praying with the sick and dying all brought many benefits to the caregiver (including a sense of oneness with the patient and of God's grace and love) and to the patient despite differences in religious tradition.[4] I certainly can agree with that assessment because that has been my experience as well. One of the more important changes in the practice of medicine in recent years has been hospice programs, which allow people who are terminally ill to be at home in the presence of loved ones and familiar surroundings. This doesn't mean that we can let all people die at home, as ideal as it may seem, because some situations require intensive surgical or medical interventions. Nevertheless, when conditions are appropriate, hospice treatment brings a new dimension to whole-patient care: a sensitivity to the physical, emotional, and spiritual needs of the patient.

The great technological advances in medical care over the past thirty years have unfortunately trained care providers to seek quick cures using the most modern (and usually expensive) bioengineering tools. Expensive medical technology is forcing medical professionals and consumers to make hard choices about health care. More and more tough decisions in health-care delivery will need to be made in the future. Many will be dictated by the high cost in tax dollars resulting from expensive procedures and diagnostic technology. Health-care providers, consumers, and ethicists must come together to develop guidelines for providing effective care without unduly high costs. Living wills, now widely in use, help maintain a patient's and his or her family's dignity in the face of death as well as limit expensive treatments when prognosis is very poor. One hopes that consideration of these issues will bring concomitantly an increased awareness of the nonphysical as well as the physical needs of the whole patient.

Our advanced technology in some ways has created a gap between the physical, emotional, and spiritual needs of the patient. The importance for the providers to just "be"—that is, to be present, sensitive, and attentive—is very important. Physicians must be present, must be sensitive to a patient's concerns, must listen, and must be aware of a patient's spiritual needs, especially as life closes slowly down. Many times the physician is forced to hand a patient over to God after exhausting all medical treatments for an illness. These skills must be learned—skills that were mastered by the old family doctor a few generations ago. Patients will often lead caregivers when dealing with spiritual matters; caregivers must learn to listen and be led instead of always trying to lead.

The still depths of the ocean are undisturbed by surface waves. Within us—in the still depths of our beings—God's spirit resides.[5]

Most of us have avoided being "boiled" by a surface wave at the seashore by diving under the wave as it breaks over us. As the wave breaks and we remain below its surface, we are barely aware of its great surface power. The hospice lends itself to the development of this particular style of caring, stressing the patient's wholeness, especially the quiet center. This could serve as a model for hospitals. Perhaps the house officers could make house calls on the hospice team to observe the interaction first-hand before finding themselves the attending doctors. It takes a fair amount of experience to just "be" with a dying patient, but these visits are worth whatever uneasiness a physician might experience. Through this experience professional caregivers are made aware of their impotence as they recognize that they are unable to heal. They feel that they have failed. But some conditions are beyond cure, and people will die despite everything medical science can do. Understanding death as part of life's cycle and as part of medical practice is often difficult and frightening. Even now I often experience the death of a patient as a personal loss and must remind myself that it is part of life and medicine. Dorothy C. H. Ley and Inge B. Corless define spiritual care as "the art of communicating the love of God to persons at their point of need."[6] They go on to say that spiritual needs are not to be confused with religious needs and that all individuals have their own innate spirituality. The members of the hospice team must not divide the patient into specialized compartments, but should treat the patient as a unit. Each member "must be able to draw from their spiritual well to satisfy the patients' needs and the needs of the members of the team. Everyone must take the time to just be."[7]

A Ventilator, a Sick Patient, and God's Answer to Prayer

God always answers prayer, but in his own way. Steve was a seventy-two-year-old retired teacher whom I'd known for only a few years. He suffered from severe heart failure, his heart being nearly the size of a volleyball and barely working. His blood pressure was 95/60 on a "good day" (very low pressure for a large man). Because of this, he quickly became out of breath when performing even the mildest form of exercise. He was an upbeat individual, and I did my best at every office visit to give him hope and encouragement. The day finally came when he required hospitalization. He needed what appeared to be the short-term use of a ventilator to breathe properly. Several days passed, and while being weaned off the ventilator, he suffered a stroke rendering him comatose. It soon became apparent that he would not survive. His devoted wife found it very difficult to give permission to remove the ventilator, though she knew that it was the right decision, as Steve had indicated this choice in his living will. One Sunday afternoon she called and said that the next morning she would like to be present with other family members as we removed the ventilator. I knew what a traumatic experience this was for her. So I prayed after our telephone conversation that the Lord would intercede in some way. Two hours later, the phone rang, and it was the nurse at the hospital stating that Steve had passed quietly away. Needless to say, though all concerned were sorry that this fine person had died, a wonderful peace came to Steve's wife and family. It was the Lord who interceded and in his mercy spared the despair and guilt that would have crushed Steve's wife. She would otherwise have had to live with that painful decision the rest of her life. The Lord had taken Steve, who was already brain-dead. We accepted this with relief and thankful hearts. Decisions to remove life support are made every day, and it is always an emotionally difficult choice even when there is a living will. In this case, the spouse, who was completely overwhelmed, was spared the additional trauma.

Postoperative Loss of Speech and Paralysis

Mary was admitted to the hospital with recurring, transient small strokes. Her workup revealed that she had a brain aneurysm that was leaking and could rupture at any time with devastating results. Mary, an accountant, was only fifty-five years old and a very active and alert mother of two teenage children. We often had prayed together on other occasions in the office and did so as she was about to undergo brain surgery. The surgery was successful, but, on the evening of the same day, the surgeon called to say that Mary was alert but had lost her speech and the ability to move on her right side. I was crushed! I was up most of that night praying that the Lord would help her recover. The next morning I held my breath as I walked into the intensive care unit. Tears of joy came to my eyes as she waved with her right arm and said, "Hello Bill!" Her speech had obviously returned and so had the use of her right arm and leg! Evidently a spasm of the circulation had occurred in the early postoperative period of the surgery, but it was now gone. God hears our prayers, but he answers them according to his will.

Not all cases, however, end so happily. At times, one can be faced with a long journey of rehabilitation and many days of prayer. Progress may be painfully slow.

> My child, when you come to serve the Lord,
> prepare yourself for testing.
> Set your heart right and be steadfast,
> and do not be impetuous in time of calamity.
> Cling to him and do not depart,
> so that your last days may be prosperous.
> Accept whatever befalls you,
> and in times of humiliation be patient.
> For gold is tested in the fire,
> and those found acceptable, in the furnace of humiliation.
> Trust in him, and he will help you;
> make your ways straight, and hope in him.
>
> –Sirach 2:1–6

Further Reading

Brother Roger of Taizé, *Parable of Community* (Oxford: A. R. Mowbray and Co., 1984).

Taizé, an ecumenical community started in 1940 by Brother Roger in the hills outside Burgundy, France, is a remarkable place to visit. The book explains the Rule of Taizé and the day-to-day working environment of this loving and unique Christian community. The community has gradually grown so that there are now more than eighty Catholic and Protestant brothers from over twenty countries.

In 1966 a congregation of Catholic sisters from a nearby village, following the techniques of Saint Ignatius of Loyola, began welcoming visitors from all over the world. Dozens of large tents house the young people who come. Rooms for guests who prefer not to stay in a tent are also available. Accommodations are sparse but the hospitality overcomes any lack of special amenities.

The community offers three services consisting of chanting and singing in various languages that attract a large number of participants, especially college-age students. Separate multilanguage discussion groups relating to lifestyle, beliefs, and spirituality are also offered. On any given weekend in the summer several thousand young people gather there.

3

Some Frequent Signs of the Aging Process

One of the problems frequently associated with advancing age is decreased oxygen intake by our body tissues. This means that as we age there is a steady fall in our endurance. Studies show that, with regular exercise, this natural decrease in "our wind" for strenuous work can be slowed, and in some cases can even be equal to another individual's performance who may be twenty years younger. I will say more about this later.

Decreased flexibility is another well-known result of aging. A few years ago, after returning from a weekend swimming camp for Masters swimmers, I realized that I no longer was able to touch my toes. This was just one of several stretching drills, none of which I did well. Then one day several weeks later, after practicing diligently the various stretching exercises, I felt like a kid again when I exclaimed to my wife that I had touched my toes! I had lost a great deal of back flexibility insidiously over the years and never really knew it.

Decreased hearing is another one of nature's bad tricks that seems to come upon us unannounced, and, for most of us, there doesn't seem to be any precipitating cause.

Deafness: An Instant Cure

One outstanding example of healing, which occurred in my office a few years ago and concerned Barney, a forty-nine-year-old professor, was the exception to the rule. Barney's chief complaint was that he needed a hearing aid. Noting that he was still in his forties, I remarked that he was a bit young for that. Nevertheless he replied that he had great difficulty hearing the students sitting around the table in a seminar he conducted, and he also described the greatly reduced hearing loss he experienced while in China during a six-month sabbatical. He was certain he needed a hearing aid. So I looked into his left ear, and, to our mutual surprise, I promptly removed a cotton ball! I then looked into the other ear and removed a cotton plug from that one as well! To his astonishment, he suddenly could hear! It was a miracle! An instant cure! (There are not too many instant cures in the practice of medicine, and I quickly pointed this fact out to him.) I asked him if he had been seen by an ear doctor recently. He quickly replied that he hadn't. But then he suddenly gasped as he searched back in his memory and said in an astonished voice, his face turning red, "You know, a year ago last Thanksgiving I did see an ear doctor. He said to come back in a few days, but I felt so much better I didn't return." We both laughed at this "miraculous cure" as he left the office that day. But, as I said, this is rarely the cause of deafness.

Perhaps 60 percent of people over the age of sixty-five have some hearing loss; this figure rises to 90 percent in those over eighty.[1] Most cases result from aging of the inner ear parts, the eighth nerve, the brainstem pathways, or the brain itself. Other conditions besides aging, including infections and certain medications, can cause or aggravate hearing loss. Constant exposure to loud noise can also lead to deafness. Federal agencies have set 85 decibels as the level above which hearing damage may occur. Normal speaking is usually in the 50-decibel range while a rock band may generate 120 decibels; this is loud enough that instant hearing loss has been reported after unprotected exposure, according to Steven R. Gambert and Krishan Gupta.[2] Laborers may also be exposed to loud noises. Fortunately, ear covering devices are worn more frequently than in prior years among workers near noisy machines. Some of the medications that may be responsible for hearing loss when used over long periods of time and in high doses are aspirin, quinine, furosemide, vancomycin, and indomethacin. (Although quinine has been used for decades to prevent nocturnal leg cramps caused by poor circulation, the mechanism of action is not understood. Furosemide is a diuretic. Vancomycin is an antibiotic used in the treatment of various conditions, including colitis caused by toxin-producing bacteria resulting from prolonged use of a number of other antibiotics. Indomethacin is a noncortisone anti-inflammatory agent useful for many conditions, including arthritis, bursitis, and pericanditis.)

Once the need for a hearing aid is established, it is a good idea to spend time with an audiologist to learn listening techniques and how to take care of the aid as well as to hear some words of encouragement or advice. The majority of people with hearing aids use a small device that fits in the ear and is more appealing cosmetically than the older, larger models.

Hearing is very important to us. We must be able to communicate with others. Decreased hearing can strain relationships and can interfere with medical treatment as well as the enjoyment of lectures, music, and many other pleasurable things in our environment.

It is very difficult to be a disciple, to reach out to others, when you have little or no hearing, no matter what your status. The following has been one of my favorite meditations for the past several years:

> The Lord GOD has given me a well-trained tongue,
> that I might know how to speak to the weary a word that
>   will rouse them.
> Morning after morning he opens my ear that I may hear;
> And I have not rebelled, not turned back.
>
> –Isaiah 50:4–5

After reading this passage it struck me that perhaps Isaiah should have a special place of honor for ear, nose, and throat specialists. Even so, hearing God speak to us with our hearts can be experienced by all of us—including those who are hearing impaired.

Decreased balance and fear of falling is another problem frequently encountered with advancing age. One may have difficulty turning quickly from left to right or looking up suddenly. A wide-based gait and a hesitancy in getting up out of a chair and walking often develops in older people. However, these individuals still need a thorough checkup by their physician as one can easily be fooled that this behavior is "normal" when one gets older and should therefore be ignored.

An Unsteady Old Man: Something to Be Expected?

Henry is a lovely retired seventy-five-year-old C.P.A. who had an overabundance of good health until he developed an unsteadiness that ultimately led to a bed- and chair-bound existence. A routine CAT scan of the head revealed excess fluid accumulation in the brain. There is a surgical procedure in which a shunt is constructed to drain away excess fluid from the brain and thereby relieve increased pressure. This surgery was suggested, but Henry said he had lived long enough, and he refused further treatment. Family members nagged him so much that he finally agreed to the procedure. I had known Henry only after he was mostly bedbound— curled up in the fetal position, lethargic, and barely responsive. The change in him after the surgery was one of the most spectacular transformations I have ever witnessed! A few short months following surgery he was alert, walking without a cane, bright as a tack, and telling family members to hurry up and get him to physiotherapy as he had a lot of things to do that day. Normal pressure hydrocephalus is the term used to describe this type of condition. Gait disturbances may also be caused by side effects from medications, vitamin B-12 deficiency, and Parkinson's disease. Arthritis and muscular weakness or other abnormalities including strokes can also be responsible for difficulties in getting about. It is estimated that about one fourth of the cases of gait disturbances arise from treatable conditions.[3] A number of nursing homes institute daily leg muscle–building programs for very old patients in an attempt to show that function can be improved. After a number of months of intensive exercises, many patients exhibited improved walking ability and balance (some patients even started dancing again). This success encourages all concerned to search for other causes of gait disturbances rather than accepting them as part of the "normal aging process." To see these patients renew their interest in their environment, to be interested in physically getting about, and to exhibit a reawakened spirituality is a source of great joy for both the patients and those taking care of them; the body temple has become whole again.

Insomnia in the Elderly

Sleep disorders are common among the elderly. A number of medical conditions can cause or aggravate insomnia in this population group. Lung conditions such as asthma and emphysema can interfere with sleep. Other painful conditions such as peptic ulcers and arthritis can also inhibit sleep. Pain seems worse during the night. Frequent urination caused by an enlarged prostate or uncontrolled diabetes can interfere with sleep. At times congestive heart failure will cause shortness of breath at night when the patient, who has concomitant edema of the legs, lies down, and the fluid from his or her swollen legs overloads the lungs. General depression and anxiety and worry over such issues as nursing home placement and socioeconomic changes accompanying the aging process all can result in insomnia. I have often noted that, at medical conferences, the senior doctors (who probably have some trouble sleeping) often are the first to nod off when the lights go out for a slide presentation. With that in mind and having reached the status of senior attending physician myself, I now make heroic efforts to stay awake. But I feel somewhat consoled when I note a few young house officers, who have been up a good part of the night, also sleeping soundly when the lights are dimmed. Researchers studying insomnia in the elderly find the following helpful: use the bed only for sleeping (not for leisure time); avoid caffeine, alcohol, tobacco, and large meals before going to bed; and make sure the bedroom is at a comfortable temperature. They also suggest performing daily exercise, avoiding naps, and going to bed and getting up at the same time each day.[4] Try to confine worry to the daytime and read or listen to music prior to sleeping. Exposure to bright light during the day can enhance nighttime sleep. Earplugs and eye shades may also be helpful. Snoring is frequently caused by sleeping on the back and thus can be helped by sewing a golf or tennis ball in the back of the pajamas so that, when the individual rolls on his or her back and begins to snore, this unpleasant bump will cause the individual to roll over to the side. Certain medications used to treat acute confusion (senility) such as propanalol, reserpine, alcohol, and levodopa have occasionally caused nightmares and may have to be eliminated in order to ensure proper sleeping.

Chronic insomnia, so common among the elderly, is often associated with fatigue during the day. The difficulty in treating the insomnia is that long-term use of sleeping pills can result in tolerance and habituation, which, in turn, can lead paradoxically to drug-induced insomnia.[5] Remember, alcohol and sleep medications do not mix!

Sporadic insomnia, however, may not be all that bad. Sometimes while lying in bed at night, the answer to a difficult problem becomes clearer. I've often felt that the Lord used this time to speak to me. His still, small voice comes through unmistakably at this time, more so than during the hectic daylight hours. When the dawn breaks, I begin the new day with an inner peace; the Lord is at work on the matter, and an answer materializes.

> My presence will go with you,
> and I will give you rest.
> –Exodus 33:14

The Aging Heart and Coronary Arteries

The left ventricle becomes stiffer with increasing age because of increased thickness. This thickness is thought to be a response to the narrowing of the body's arteries caused by the buildup of cholesterol plaque, not unlike the accumulation of soap in the kitchen pipes with each passing year. The heart must work harder to circulate the blood because of the narrowed vessel lumens (cavities). This is why systolic blood pressure (the upper blood pressure number) may rise. It is like the increased water pressure passing through the garden hose when one turns the nozzle. The left atrium, when contracting to force the blood into the stiff left ventricle, will often make a heart sound, which the physician can hear with a stethoscope and which is called a fourth heart sound. Atrial fibrillation (the atria may beat about 300 beats per minute and the ventricles, or pulse, may beat about 150 beats per minute) is about twice as common in the elderly. Various types of conduction delays of the heartbeat from the atrium to the ventricles are also more common with age. If the pulse is too slow, an artificial pacemaker is often implanted.

A New Pacemaker and a New Life

George was a retired seventy-eight-year-old high school teacher who was engaged to a charming seventy-three-year-old part-time secretary. A problem occurred when George experienced a number of near-fainting spells during their courtship, one notable time while sipping wine during a romantic candlelight dinner. The cause was a heartbeat that had become too slow (at times as low as 30 beats per minute). This often happens as we age. A permanent cardiac pacemaker was put in place that was set to trigger whenever George's own heart rate fell below 68 beats per minute, which solved the problem. Following his permanent pacemaker implantation, the wedding plans went forward with joy and confidence.

An Unforgettable Farewell Dinner

Irving was the guest of honor at a retirement dinner given by the bank where he had been employed as an executive for thirty years. He was a good tennis player and had excellent health habits. His blood pressure was on the low side because of his years of exercise and trim physique. After a large dinner, one glass of wine, and a long time sitting at the table, he was finally introduced and invited to come up to the podium. Irving suddenly stood up, took two steps, and promptly fell on his face. Fortunately, he didn't hurt himself. In a few seconds he was up and speaking; the only injury was to his dignity. The combination of standing up quickly (gravity tends to decrease the blood pressure), a large meal (there is a pooling of the circulation in the gut when we digest), and a glass of wine (alcohol can dilate the arteries, causing a fall in blood pressure)—all this in a man with low normal blood pressure who probably was fatigued at the end of a long day—resulted in Irving's fainting spell. Although not serious, it did illustrate what is meant by postural hypotension (fainting when one suddenly stands up too quickly), which occurs more frequently in the elderly.

Heart strain without chest pains (silent angina) also increases with age. Eugene L. Coodley and co-workers found a 20 percent prevalence of silent angina among those sixty to sixty-nine-years-old and a 36 percent prevalence among those seventy or older.[6] Because a person may not note any chest discomfort when exercising and thus not have any warning that he or she is straining the heart and may therefore fail to slow down or stop. A stress test is one way to catch this condition before it's too late.

The amount of work the heart performs, the cardiac output, falls about 1 percent per year on the average. But the decrease in efficiency of the heart can often be delayed with age by making certain lifestyle changes. The precursors of coronary artery arteriosclerosis are found especially among young boys in the Western world at a very early age, often when not yet adolescents. Depending frequently on each individual's lifestyle as he or she ages, fatty streaks lining the coronary arteries develop into progressively enlarging deposits of cholesterol over the years, leading to coronary artery blockages or narrowings that can cause pain or lead to a heart attack. After menopause, women lose the heart-protecting effect of estrogen and soon catch up with men in the incidence of coronary artery disease. This, of course, is the argument for giving some postmenopausal women estrogen. Other benefits for giving estrogen to women are protection against osteoporosis, the easing of hot flashes, and the maintenance of secondary sex characteristics (such as youthful appearance, smooth skin, lack of excess facial hair).

The condition of the coronary arteries of average individuals is influenced by the society and era in which they live. For example, during the Korean War, 75 percent of American soldiers age twenty-two were found to have coronary artery disease when their hearts were examined after they had been killed, though virtually none of the enemy soldiers had it.[7] With the greater emphasis upon exercise and better health habits twenty years later, the repeat studies done upon American soldiers killed during the Vietnam War revealed a 50 percent incidence of coronary artery disease.[8] More recently there has been a further drop in coronary artery disease among males in the United States. There has also been a steady decrease in tobacco consumption in the U.S. among boys and adult males. However, no corresponding decrease in cigarette consumption has taken place among girls and women. Cigarette smoking can override the heart-protective effect of estrogen present in premenopausal women. Lung cancer has surpassed breast cancer in postmenopausal women as the number one cancer.

Estrogen can help to protect postmenopausal women from heart attacks. On the other hand, estrogen may stimulate the growth of breast or uterine tumors. I encountered a postmenopausal woman recently in the office who walks two miles every day (thus helping bone formation in her spine and lower extremities), takes calcium daily, has low blood cholesterol and excellent blood pressure, and doesn't smoke. She opted not to take estrogen at this time in her life, and I agreed with her. If a woman had fibroids of the uterus or multiple breast cysts or a strong family history of breast cancer, I would be inclined not to prescribe estrogen for her either. There are other people who fit somewhere between these two cases and I usually consult with a gynecologist in order to make the best decision. Above all, the patient must feel comfortable with taking estrogen for this to be recommended. Even though women are generally protected from heart attacks by their own estrogens before menopause, should a woman suffer a heart attack for any reason, she is twice as likely as a man to die in the first year after the attack. Perhaps because their coronary arteries are smaller than their male counterparts', angioplasty (balloon dilation) of a coronary artery is often not as successful in women. For men, heart disease becomes the number one cause of death starting at age forty while in women it is number one around sixty-five.

Nevertheless, even young women can have heart attacks, especially if they have many of the risk factors: cigarette smoking, diabetes, high blood cholesterol, high-density cholesterol (HDL, the "good" cholesterol) values below 40 mg. %, high blood pressure, stress, obesity, lack of aerobic exercise, and a strong family history of heart disease. Certain risk factors are additive; for example, young, premenopausal women who smoke and use oral contraceptives have ten times the risk of cardiac mortality than those who neither smoke nor use oral contraceptives.[9] Very frequently a middle-aged or elderly male patient will ask whether the nasty argument he had with his boss within the past few days brought on his heart attack. That is not likely. In most cases it seems, a heart attack is the culmination of many years of cholesterol deposits in the coronary arteries resulting in a narrowing of the lumens of these vessels and ultimately ending in a thrombosis (blockage) of one particular vessel.

The more frequently the heart attacks occur, the more the heart heals with a scar. Unlike normal tissue, scars do not contain the elastic fibers responsible for normal cardiac contraction. Thus the ventricle is no longer able to squeeze properly, which can result in heart failure, rhythm disturbances (palpitations of a more serious type), and fatigue. Now because of better treatment, heart patients are living longer, though often with restricted lifestyles and requiring frequent attention. Some heart patients are candidates for heart transplantation. I will discuss this option further in chapter 14.

In the 1940s Ancel Keyes noted that malnutrition led to a slowing of the heart rate, poor appetite, and fatigue. This can be a vicious circle: poor nutrition, lowered serum protein, loss of body tissue, loss of weight, drug toxicity, further loss of appetite, and progression of malnutrition with additional weight loss. Problems associated with aging such as delayed liver metabolism of medications, delayed kidney excretion, and drug interactions all add up to the possibility for drug toxicity and heart malfunction. For example, taking certain arthritis drugs together results in the retention of fluid, which can cause heart failure in certain circumstances.

Though there are many causes for heart disease, coronary artery disease is the number one killer. It is also the heart disease over which we have the most control. One important way to control coronary artery disease is to avoid tobacco. My colleagues, who perform cardiac catheterizations (procedures to view the condition of someone's coronary arteries) on a daily basis, have found that smoking can age the coronary arteries by as much as fifteen years. I will cover this in some detail in the following chapter.

Further Reading

David Reuben, Thomas T. Yoshikawa, and Richard Besdine, eds., *Geriatrics Review: A Core Curriculum in Geriatric Medicine* (New York: American Geriatrics Society, 1993–94).

Geriatrics Review is an excellent journal exploring the medical aspects of hearing loss, gait disturbances, sleep disorders, dementia, and delirium, to name a few of the topics.

4

Cultivating and Maintaining a Healthy Lifestyle

Teen Years

What habits should we adopt, beginning as teenagers, to help preserve the body temple? What issues should we consider when making lifestyle decisions? During my office visits with teenagers, I strongly advise them to adopt six habits that will pay off all their lives, from their teenage years to midlife to old age. These habits are avoiding tobacco, doing some form of aerobic exercise daily, avoiding drug use and alcohol abuse, acting responsible sexually, setting aside quiet time to slow down from life's frenetic pace, and cultivating a good self-image.

Avoid Tobacco

There are many diseases and disabilities related to tobacco use—one effect that can be noted, even in teenagers, is increased susceptibility to respiratory infections and asthma. Lung function decreases with tobacco use, and over time this decrease can lead to pulmonary emphysema. Cancer of the lung is almost always associated with tobacco use, as are most cases of coronary artery disease and diminished circulation to the extremities. The recent recognition that nonsmoking bystanders are also susceptible to the above conditions through secondhand smoke reveals the illness pattern to be much more widespread than previously believed. Athletic participation, good peer role models, and the smoking (or non-smoking) habits of parents all influence the teenager's decision to use tobacco or not. It is important to know that most adult smokers began the habit before age twenty-one.

Perform Aerobic Exercise Regularly

Aerobic exercise is perhaps the second most influential factor in developing good health habits. Virtually no cross-country runners are smokers, for example. More will be noted about regular aerobic exercise in chapter 9.

Avoid Drug and Alcohol Abuse

Drug and alcohol abuse are extremely harmful to the body temple. For example, cocaine can cause sudden cardiac arrest, tremors, convulsions, and breathing abnormalities. Marijuana can cause confusion and memory loss. PCP, heroin, LSD, amphetamines, barbituates, and also prescription drugs when used improperly can cause irreparable damage to the body. Illicit drug use is illegal and thus can lead to arrest and imprisonment, which is also harmful to the body temple. Unfortunately, we have all read in the paper about or know of someone who has been killed or harmed by drugs.

Alcohol abuse damages the liver and the brain. Both alcohol and drug abuse often lead to malnutrition and a compromised immune system.

Be Responsible Sexually

Being irresponsible sexually can often lead to sexually transmitted diseases, including gonorrhea, syphilis, and AIDS. Sexual promiscuity also damages one's emotional health. Misuse of sex undermines the binding relationship that lovemaking affirms.

Abuse of alcohol, drugs, or sex can lead to serious damage to one's emotional and spiritual as well as physical health.

Set Aside Quiet Time

Will the courts allow schoolchildren to experience a quiet time at the start of the school day? Children seem to have precious little time today to walk in the woods or read a book that's not a required text, and the time they do have is filled with violence on TV, listening to music on a Walkman or portable radio—so much noise and reluctance (fear?) to be alone with themselves. Parents have a hard time also finding time for a bedtime story for their children. It doesn't always get better in one's middle years when life can be even more demanding of free time. The clergy have as much difficulty as we do in finding time to read scripture daily. I remember a continual education course for pastors in which participants were asked how many of them spent fifteen minutes a day in prayer and only a small number raised their hands. We all need time with the Lord, time to calm down. Starting at a young age paves the way for incorporating this discipline into one's life.

Developing a basis of spirituality is vital, and lucky are the parents who have the ability to strike this sensitive note in children when they are still young. Setting aside quiet time has physical, as well as emotional and spiritual benefits, in the form of an improved immune response. Lack of such stress-relieving time can result in a host of medical problems. A moral structure or code also is very important, although religion per se may not develop until later. At times it is well into midlife, when one is placed between a rock and a hard place, before the need for prayers and a worshiping community is welcomed.

The Gallup Youth Survey has been conducting surveys among teens for the past sixteen years. Only 43 percent of teens feel that it is vital to have solid religious beliefs, but nearly all teens believe in God or a Supreme Being according to the survey. A caring attitude among teens is reflected in the 66 percent who are actively involved in helping others in the community.[1] During Orientation Week for incoming freshmen at Princeton University, when faced with the option of camping or working on inner-city projects (painting, carpentry work, etc.), the new students overwhelmingly chose the latter.

As teens mature, settle down, begin to raise a family, and enter middle age, the role of spirituality becomes increasingly more apparent. When asked how important religion is in their lives, 46 percent of those under thirty, 54 percent of those between thirty and forty-nine, and 70 percent of those fifty or older said it was "very important."[2]

Maintain a Good Self-Image

Not only children but adults also need to be reaffirmed or recognized as special people at regular intervals throughout their lives. It takes only a moment to tell someone how much you appreciate them; believe me, we all need this at any age.

My mother tutored children at home. I remember her reading to one student at a time as they sat around the dining-room table. I could hear her say over and over again, "That's wonderful Henry!" or "Angie, you are doing so well!" The children loved my mother because she was a good teacher but also because she built up their confidence and self-image in the process. My father died when I was twelve, and, when we were dealing with a paucity of finances, she would say, "No matter what happens, remember you are a Haynes." She made me feel that I was something special. Whatever "being a Haynes" meant was never spelled out, but it helped to create a good self-image for me that made me feel warm inside.

One's self-image affects one's physical health as well in that confidence and outgoingness help us meet physical challenges. The positive affect of peace of mind on the immune system is another byproduct of good self-image.

The power of motivation is also very important. The well-motivated young person with a good image of his or her self-worth is very fortunate. This person, armed with a good home or other affirming support system, is well on the way to a productive life as an adult. Success in so many avenues of life seems to revolve around motivation and persistence. One need not be a genius. Given an average intelligence, I feel one's MQ (Motivation Quotient) may very well be more important than one's IQ (Intelligence Quotient) in determining success.

Middle and Later Years

Mental deterioration can be avoided to a certain extent in the middle and later years of life by keeping active with hobbies, social groups, or other activities.

My father-in-law belonged to three different men's luncheon groups. Each met on a different day of the week. He kept his small office even after he retired and regularly went there to follow the stock market. He continued to read business journals and managed to play golf with friends regularly—all this into his eighties. My grandfather practiced medicine for over fifty years and even saw five patients the day he died at age eighty-seven. My high school swimming coach, Mickey Vogt, still swims daily, competes in his age-group meets across the country, and is employed by a swim club in the summer to teach children how to swim. He is eighty-eight and looks twenty years younger. The point is that, regardless of one's age, keeping in the mainstream of life, being with people, and keeping interested in what is going on in the world has a positive effect. Keeping active, if by God's grace you can, can prevent isolation, depression, and mental sluggishness.

Perhaps being more in tune with our own finiteness and the fact that we are not going to live forever will encourage us to turn to spiritual concerns in our later years. Ideally we should set aside a daily quiet time that includes prayer, meditation, and contemplation. Membership in a community of believers (or some religious affiliation), scripture reading, and keeping a daily journal of victories, frustrations, prayers, or meaningful events are also important aspects of one's spirituality. I must confess that I was well into midlife before I came to this realization. But for the past twelve years, I have been very diligent in following a routine of prayer and journal keeping every morning for twenty to thirty minutes. It has been nothing short of God's grace that has allowed me this priceless time with him in the early part of the day. It has been of untold blessings to me. Meditation on a daily basis enables one to begin the day with an inner peace. My meditation time has a definite beginning and a definite end and is always performed in the same quiet place at home. The peace derived from the time spent in quiet meditation can then be brought into the workplace. By practicing God's presence all day, I can tackle life's problems and complexities with a contemplative peace that I never before thought possible. In contrast to meditation, contemplation, in my view, has no boundaries or limits, no beginning and no ending, but consists of experiencing God's presence in all areas of living and under all conditions, stressful or joyful.

In his book *One,* Richard Bach states:

"We fly up high," I said, trembling with insight, "and we have perspective! We see every choice and fork and crossroad. But the lower we fly, the more we lose perspective. And when we land, our perspective on all other choices is gone! We focus on detail: daily hourly minutely detail, alternate lifetimes forgotten!"[3]

I understand Bach's concept, but there is another way of assessing the situation. When we center ourselves in prayer with God and quietly listen to what he is telling us, we are open to even greater vistas—his perfect plan for each of us. He will guide us, allowing us to accept new changes or opportunities. These vistas will only be limited by the love of the Father, whose love is without limit. Our decisions are more reliable when we are open to the Lord's guidance, which far surpasses human guidance. Sadly, we are often too hurried to sit still every day to listen. We don't avail ourselves of this precious time with our Lord. Laurence Freeman, O.S.B., an English priest, expresses his thoughts on the wonder of our own humanity and the amazement of the seemingly ordinary:

To be fully human means to live through time with a deepening sense of the presence of God. God is present in the present moment. If we are mindful of the here and now, awake and alert in a spirit of prayer, we live each event through infancy to old age to the fullness of our potential.[4]

If we can be present each moment, each of us will better appreciate our divine nature and God's purpose for us.

I can't emphasize too much the necessity of having a daily quiet time. Everyone needs to be present to God, to be still. Henri Nouwen agrees:

That is why I became a healer, one who can forgive, who can bring joy and peace. Not because I am totally there, but because I can go to that place in the center of my being, where I know I belong, I am safe and secure. From that place I can speak, think, act.[5]

Winifred Gallegher noted that midlife (somewhere between the ages of forty and sixty-five), instead of being a time to be dreaded, can be a pinnacle point, a new start. With the experience of overcoming life's hurdles comes a certain wisdom and acceptance of the realities of life. Those things that cannot be changed are recognized and not unduly dwelled upon, saving time and energy for new pursuits and ways to help others. Middle-aged and senior persons have an advantage over youths because wisdom cannot be fully developed while one is still a teenager or young adult.[6]

Besides the emotional and spiritual aspects, the physical component of the body temple also must be addressed during the middle and later years. In a sense, exercise is a fountain of youth, and daily exercise is very important in allowing one to remain a functioning, independent person as long as possible. Exercise is so important that I've come to the conclusion that, if one cannot exercise, it is tantamount to a cardiac—even an entire body—emergency. Think what can go wrong when one can't walk because of, for example, acute arthritis of the knee: body weight goes up causing weight-bearing joints to suffer; blood pressure and cholesterol increases; endorphin (an enzyme that gives one a sense of well-being) production decreases; stress level goes up as one is unable to relieve tensions; oxygen uptake efficiency decreases. Exercise makes our blood platelets less sticky (less likely to clog up our arteries); thus, lack of exercise can cause clogged arteries. Clearly, the inability to walk or exercise can have potentially serious cardiac ramifications.

Rescuing a Destroyed Body Temple

Albert, an eighty-year-old retired banker, must be included in this book because his case exemplifies the end of the line— the total collapse of the body temple in mind, body, and spirit. A hunter came upon a log cabin tucked away in the deep recesses of a nearby wood. He entered through an unlocked front door and spotted, in a corner of the room, an old man lying curled up on a couch under a bunch of old newspapers. His clothes were sullied and covered with feces and blood. The rest of the filthy room was in a total state of disarray with old bottles of whiskey and empty cans of food everywhere, dirty clothes piled in a heap, and cobwebs and dust covering the windows. The November air was chilly; the interior of the cabin was equally cold—there was no fire—and reeked from the odor of human waste. The room and its occupant undoubtedly had not been cleaned in many weeks, if not months. The hunter placed a handkerchief over his face as he stooped over the old man's body and determined that the man was still breathing but was comatose and could not be aroused. The rescue squad was called and the old man brought to the hospital, where I promptly admitted him. It was readily apparent that he was suffering from dehydration, uremia (the build-up of toxins in the blood), anemia, distended bladder, and that he had not bathed in weeks. He barely responded to a tap on his sternum, painful stimuli, or even a request to open his eyes. After he received intravenous fluids and other required treatment including transfusions, Albert was able to give us his history. He admitted that he had not seen a physician in forty years.

Over the next several days, we discovered that Albert had cancer of the colon and prostate. After another couple of weeks and a large number of medical and surgical interventions, (not to forget multiple baths, a haircut, manicure, and frequent shaves), he slowly began to blossom. He turned out to be a downright handsome gentleman. His appetite returned; he started to get up and walk with help, and, by the time he was discharged, he was alert and able to get about with minimal assistance. Someone found a pair of green plaid trousers and a brown jacket at a rummage sale, and, despite the mismatch of his outfit, he made quite a commanding exit as he waved goodbye to all the nurses the day he was discharged. He was invited to stay with a friend he had known from his days at the bank years ago. Quite an amazing transformation had taken place! Over the next few months, he began to take an interest in his environment and the world around him. Albert demonstrated one of the most impressive recoveries of the body temple I have witnessed. He soon was well enough to write a book. He began to lead a fairly active life. When he eventually died a few years later from pneumonia, he left a nonprofit institution $2 million that had remained in a bank account for many years gathering interest! Albert's is the story of a man restored (and a body temple restored) who still had much to contribute. His miraculous discovery by the hunter might be considered a divine intervention. The following scripture passages apply to Albert's situation:

> Save me, O God,
> for the waters have come up to my neck.
> I sink in deep mire, where there is not foothold;
> I have come into deep waters, and the flood sweeps
>   over me.
> I am weary with my crying;
>   my throat is parched.
> My eyes grow dim with waiting for my God.
>   –Psalm 69:1–3

> I will thank you, O Lord my God, with all my heart,
> and glorify your Name for evermore.
> For great is your love toward me;
> you have delivered me from the nethermost Pit.
>   –Psalm 86:12–13

Comments on Spirituality

It is difficult for younger people to be interested in spirituality when the coffers are full and life is bounding along apparently with little need for God. It often takes a crisis to bring a younger person to God and to force him or her to give up control and let the Lord take over. Actually, the same holds true at times for all of us, regardless of our age. In reality, we are all wounded from time to time; some wounds are greater than others. Life cannot be lived without its upsets, and no one is immune. This wounding is a constant process as we travel down life's road. Through our prayers and God's grace, we also undergo constant inner healings. We are then able to continue our journey without carrying guilt or pain. Inner healings are as important as physical healings. Although many patients can be cured of their illness, that still doesn't mean that they are healed. Inner healing is a gift of the Holy Spirit.

The Well-Meaning but Misdirected Prayer

I remember a fifty-one-year-old housewife named Marie who was recovering from surgery following the removal of her gall bladder. A well-meaning pastor visited her hospital room and promptly left after reading an uplifting passage of scripture. Marie said she appreciated the visit but wished that the pastor had asked her if she had any concerns. The surgery was the least of her worries; her major concern was for her teenage daughter who was using drugs. That was her greatest burden. Marie needed an inner healing, though the physical healing was well on its way toward completion. In my view, our psychiatric colleagues can do wonders in unraveling our memories, frequently making sense of our problems so that we can better understand and deal with our behavior. Despite these successes we may still need inner healing, no matter how much intellectual insight is gained. Even when one intellectually understands the psychodynamics of an emotional problem one may say, "I'm still hurting." Inner healing is God's grace to us. It is this inner peace that is the victory, the gem, the real prize that the Lord gives to us. Since we also know that the Lord will not speak to someone whose ears are shut, our wholeness depends on integrating all aspects of our body temple. We are thankful for all the therapies, insights, and prayers that we receive and the guidance to act on them. Psychotherapy does, indeed, play a significant role in the process of becoming a whole person. Our emotional dimension is just as important as our physical and spiritual dimensions.

If we appreciate this wonderful gift of the body temple, then we will do all we can to preserve and protect it. It is, after all, made in God's image, and it contains the kingdom of God within. If one can appreciate this as a young person, how fortunate; the healthy lifestyle started as a youngster is likely to remain healthy throughout life. It is never too late, however, to get on track. One of the most exciting aspects in the practice of medicine is witnessing the transformation (often with the physician's encouragement) of a grossly poor lifestyle to a most inspiring and healthy one. We can actually see the body temple being restored before our eyes.

Further Reading

Living with Christ (Novalis, 97 Lake Street, P.O. Box 553, Rouses Point, New York 12979-0553).

The *Living with Christ* pamphlet is published twelve times a year; each issue contains a daily mass. I have found it easier to become more familiar with scripture through organized bible study than attempt to read the entire Bible from beginning to end. In addition to *Daily Word* and the *Living Word, Living with Christ* is the third piece of literature that I use daily. The only other item I would recommend for daily use is a journal. The one I've been using is called *Daily Reminder* (Keith Clark Company), an engagement book that devotes a page to each day of the year (the year is plainly visible on the cover). I began this daily process of meditation in 1981. When the books are placed in a row on a bookshelf, one can choose any year and thus be able to track one's concerns, prayers, and victories while documenting God's presence from year to year.

5

The Mystique of Remaining Young

We Americans prefer not to transmit an elderly image of ourselves to the world. The desirability in our culture of remaining young forever is easily confirmed by the abundance of cosmetics, lotions, hair dyes, and exercise and weight-reducing programs that are meant to hold back Father Time. Currently an estimated 1.5 million Americans spend about $4 billion yearly in order to look younger and more attractive, to improve their body image, and to thus enhance their chances in a competitive labor market.

Our Aging Skin

Aging causes physical changes in our skin that result in wrinkles, spots, and other alterations. As one ages, the skin frequently takes on a paper thin quality and one loses hair and some of the skin's natural oils; thus, dryness and itching become a problem. Skin thickness may decrease by as much as 20 percent. Older skin doesn't heal as quickly as young skin because of poor circulation, poor cardiac function, or changes in the immune system that may delay healing as well as decrease the body's resistance to infection.

Further insults to our aging skin (and young image) consist of benign growths called cherry red spots or hemangiomas. Seborrheic keratoses (age spots) are common as well. (I used to call them senile keratoses until I noticed them on myself.) Rapid weight gain and loss can cause tissues to lose elasticity, which can lead to loose, excess skin folds (hanging on the arms, for example.) Hot and prolonged showers may bake the skin dry and further aggravate itching.

Alas, as we age, the male body finds itself accumulating fat around the waist and the female often notes the same process at the hips or thighs. As overall body hair decreases, some sort of conspiracy of nature makes it grow vigorously from the male's eyebrows, nostrils, and ears. Not to be outdone, the female may note increased hair production over the upper lip and on the chin.

Attaining and Maintaining a Youthful Appearance

Plastic surgery has been one approach used to attain or maintain a youthful exterior. The plastic surgeon is adept at removing fat around eyelids, tucking loose tissue under the chin, correcting ear lobes, injecting collagen into skin to fill in wrinkles, using liposuction to remove fat from the hips, reconstructing breasts to be larger or smaller, and correcting nose or jaw deformities, to name a few. The positive side to this can be a better self-image and greater self-confidence, feeling and looking healthier, and possibly enhancing one's career, especially in the case of models and actors.

Prevention of skin cancer in all ages is theoretically possible by avoiding prolonged exposure to the sun and by using an appropriate sunscreen. Wearing proper clothes that shield against the sun is important, especially during the midday hours. To lessen the appearance of lines around the eyes, try wearing sunglasses on sunny days to avoid squinting. Also avoid as much as possible very cold weather and wind, which can lead to frostbite or windburn.

Our culture calls for instant results, a quick cure, but implicit in all this desire is the need for lifestyle changes that will help maintain the gains made by the surgeon. And it must be remembered that the cosmetic change that results from the surgery will not change a person's problems and make life free from distress. The biggest concern of the plastic surgeon is to make sure the patient does not have unrealistic expectations about cosmetic surgery. Cosmetic surgery certainly is fine when a person wants to improve his or her appearance for practical reasons, such as staying in a job that demands that one remain youthful. On the other hand, some people almost accentuate their age by letting their hair turn gray or by cultivating a beard that has turned white; in essence, projecting an older appearance.

Despite our attempts to the contrary, we all continue to age. I hear frequently, "I hate getting older. My illnesses are probably due to my age." Or "It's tough being over fifty." If it's the end of a long day, I often say with a serious expression, "General Electric is making a time-reversal machine. I'm first on the list; you can be second." For a few moments, the patient may look at me with an expression of both hope and surprise. During this age of rapidly advancing technology, we tend to believe science can do most anything. When a smile crosses my face, it soon becomes apparent that I'm really joking, and alas, the bubble of make-believe has been broken; there is no such machine!

The question remains, given the choice, would any of us want to go back twenty years, even if it were possible? Don't we prefer our older children who have become "real people"? Don't we enjoy visits from grandchildren (without the day-to-day responsibilities of driving to the doctor for an earache, to ballet lessons, to back-to-school nights)? We have already traveled a fair way down life's path, perhaps have fallen a few times, and have enjoyed many of life's pleasures. The resultant gray hairs, "crow's feet," and wrinkled brow are all attractive in their own way—adding character to our faces. In the navy, we call them "hashmarks"—each group of wrinkles, like a hashmark, is worth five years' service.

Nature has a wonderful way of allowing us to see our contemporaries as at least five years older than we, that is, until we examine a recent photograph of ourselves! After all, you too may be eligible for a senior citizen discount at the movies. But there is always the hope that the person at the ticket booth won't believe you're old enough.

An Appreciation of Older Things

We live in a country that loves paradoxes. On the one hand, we oppose the federal government's interference in our lives, that is, telling us what we can and cannot do. On the other hand, we expect that same government to supply us with benefits that we perceive to be our "rights." Likewise, some of us grow up wanting someone else to take responsibility for our actions. We may turn and wave to a friend while walking down the street, for example, bump into a tree, and wonder who to blame for the abrasions that appear on our forehead. It couldn't be my fault for not looking, we tell ourselves; it must be the city's fault.

In other areas of our lives, we like old things—antiques or collector's items such as old pieces of furniture or baseball cards. But when "old" pertains to ourselves, we want nothing to do with it—we want to be youthful forever.

Many of my patients will only reluctantly reveal their true age while in midlife (including myself) but, having reached an older stage in life, will proudly announce, "In nine months, I'll be eighty-years old." Could it be that we all fear death and don't like to think of the prospect of aging? Does it remind us of our own finiteness? At some point, though, toward the end of the journey, most of us are able to accept aging as a normal part of life and, hence, are no longer preoccupied with the youth culture.

Nevertheless, we are all different, and that is probably a saving grace for society. Maintaining a youthful attitude and doing the best with what God has given us can lead to a reasonably healthy lifestyle and goad us to treasure the body temple a bit more. The drive to remain youthful and productive has much to say for itself, even though no two people will approach their situation the same way. A point made by Thomas Moore in his book *Care of the Soul* reminds me that not all that is old is necessarily bad:

Ruins, like old farm equipment in my neighbor's pastures, show us that something remains of beauty in a thing when its function has departed. Soul is then revealed, as though it had been hidden for years under well-oiled functioning. Soul is not about function, it is about beauty and form and memory.[1]

6

The Rapidly Aging Population

B elieve it or not, the fastest growing population segment in the United States during the next decade will be composed of those over eighty-five. This group encompasses 2.6 million people and will grow to double that figure by the year 2000.[1] Though the average lifespan of Westerners is now around seventy-four years, many are living well into their eighties and nineties. Thus, one of medicine's and society's problems is to help the elderly to function better in order to minimize medical and nursing costs and, at the same time, to increase this group's quality of life. Some authors use the term *active life* expectancy to express functioning well and with a sense of well-being. Instead of using the yardstick of death to calculate life expectancy, they prefer to measure the level at which people can function along the "activities of daily living" (ADL) scale. This method is especially helpful in dealing with noninstitutionalized people for purposes of planning and overall handling of the problems of aging.[2]

Since the elderly use a third of the hospital beds, a fourth of the prescribed medications, and 27 percent of the health-care dollars expended in the U.S., an increasing need to incorporate this group of individuals into our teaching programs, as well as medical planning strategies, is necessary. The amount of hospitalizations due to adverse drug reactions is 50 percent higher in the elderly than in those below sixty years of age. One researcher found that, with the same dosage, the amount of the drug diazepam was two times higher in the blood stream of an eighty-year-old than in that of a thirty-year-old individual.[3] The level in the blood of many medications is influenced by the serum albumin (blood protein), which is often decreased in the elderly. Lower serum albumin decreases binding, which leads to an increased level of the drug in the blood. Higher levels of the drug can lead to toxicity.

The more numerous the medications prescribed, the more likely is the possibility of a drug side effect or adverse reaction. Research pharmacologist Allen F. Shaughnessy reported that the possibility of drug complications is 6 percent with two drugs given together, 50 percent with five, and possibly 100 percent with eight or more drugs.[4]

In general, men die younger than women. When asked by a colleague in the audience why the life expectancy for women is longer than for men (about eight years longer), Dr. John W. Rowe suggested that perhaps men kill themselves off sooner, tobacco being the most likely offending agent. He found that 45 percent of the mortality could be attributed to coronary artery disease and 15 percent to lung cancer and emphysema, both of these largely influenced by smoking. Suicides and accidents accounted for another 15 percent of the differences in male over female mortality.[5]

Types of Aging

Actual age is often a poor criterion for determining whether an individual is "old." The following three categories are helpful in assessing someone's age.[6]

1. Biological aging: biochemical and hormonal changes occurring over time that one cannot control. This may be the nearest thing to "normal" aging.

2. Psychological aging: adapting to changes in one's life, including painful hurts, accidents, and crippling illnesses. I would include a spiritual component in this category. This component would reflect the degree that one has experienced inner healing from wounds that can compound the problems of aging.

3. Sociological aging: changes in family interconnections and economic circumstances and potential loss of friends, interests, and community activities. I have seen the difficult situation of an elderly parent moving from his or her roots to a new location to live with a well-intentioned daughter or son. Those who are fortunate enough to find a retirement community in which they are able to function well with new friends of similar age seem to fare somewhat better. But so often many of these "ideal" situations are neither possible nor practical.

Without strong roots, people can have greater difficulty with aging. The poor and homeless are daily reminders of the difficulty of coping, especially when older. Their body temples frequently are broken into many fragments. In this era of oppression, greed, job layoffs, hunger, and increasing violence in our cities, the following psalm seems appropriate:

"Why, O Lord, do you stand far off?
Why do you hide yourself in times of trouble?
In arrogance the wicked persecute the poor,—
let them be caught in the schemes they have devised.
For the wicked boast of the desires of their heart,
those greedy for gain curse and renounce the Lord.
In the pride of their countenance the wicked say, "God
will not seek it out";
all their thoughts are, "There
is no God."
                                        —Psalm 10:1–4

A Homeless Man on the Streets of New York

One of my old friends, Peter, told this story of a recent visit to Manhattan, where he was upset by the large number of poor, homeless, and mentally ill or disabled individuals who approached him along every block he walked. From prior experiences, he always carried several dollar bills in his outside pockets that he could readily give when approached by one of these poor souls. He soon noted how rapidly he was dispensing these dollars, as there seemed to be an endless stream of poor people asking for a handout. Finally, he realized that he had only one dollar left. He decided that he would ask the very next poor soul that approached him to do him a favor. Soon after making this resolve, he encountered perhaps the most needy person he had seen all day. The man looked to be somewhere between fifty-five and seventy years old, had rags for clothes, and was unshaven, thin, depressed, malnourished, and apparently devoid of any earthly possessions. The beggar approached him with downcast eyes and asked, "Can you give me something for a bowl of soup?" Peter replied, "If you first do me a favor." The beggar was stunned. Here was a man, Peter, who had actually stopped and engaged him in conversation and, in addition, had asked him for a favor. "Me, do you a favor?" he said raising his eyes up to look at Peter. "What can a poor man with no money do for you?" Peter calmly looked at him and replied, "Pray for me." The beggar looked astonished and said, "Right here on the street corner?" Peter said, "Yes." So the old man raised up his right arm to the heavens and placed the other on Peter's shoulder. As he started to pray out loud, his downtrodden demeanor slowly began to change. Slowly but surely his face was transformed. Peter noted a definite glow that was previously absent, and with each passing moment the man's voice became stronger, even vibrant. A beautiful smile came across the stranger's face. At the conclusion of the prayer, Peter thanked him, handed over his dollar, and went on his way. Before turning the corner, he looked back and saw that the man was still smiling as he gazed upward, evidently still praying as both arms were now lifted to the heavens.

One cannot help but notice that, although the poor man had no material things to give to Peter, he gave his only and undoubtedly most precious gift: God's love. The poor man likewise received a blessing, as is so often the case when we pray, since both the one praying and the receiver of the prayer share in God's grace. Peter had stopped and talked to this man and had recognized him as a child of God. He had accepted this man's gift of prayer with gratitude. I believe that God intervenes by interjecting certain people into our lives who, though total strangers, may save our lives or change them for the better. Could this encounter have been that sort of intervention? I don't know, but I am open to that possibility and pray that it touched that homeless man. Perhaps this was a turning point for him. Let's pray about this.

> Look to him, and be radiant; so your faces shall never
>   be ashamed.
> This poor soul cried, and was heard by the Lord, and was
>   saved from every trouble.
> The angel of the Lord encamps around those who fear
>   him, and delivers them.
> O taste and see that the Lord is good;
> happy are those who take refuge in him.
>
> –Psalm 34:5–8

The following, written by Jean Vanier, struck me in the context of Peter's brief encounter with the poor man.

> As we enter into a living relationship with the poor, we discover the contemplative dimension of love—how Jesus is hidden in the heart of the weak; how the face of the poor is the reflection of the face of Jesus.[7]

In a sermon preached at Trinity Church in Princeton, New Jersey, Reverend Bruce M. Webber noted, "You don't have to live in Camden or Trenton or New York to come into contact with someone penniless, hungry, dirty, crying, smelly, abusive, self-abusing, helpless." He went on to say that Jesus calls all of the human family into a relationship, with no exclusions; this relationship can be a healing for all of us. The poor we would rather step over and avoid are the very ones that will lead us into a community of healing relationships. Bruce continued, "We have lost our soul. We keep trying to fill up with all the things Jesus has warned us about. We grab, consume, fill, control."[8] We all need healing, not just on a personal level, but at a community level as well. By looking into the painful expression of the hurting poor and homeless we will see the face of Jesus.

Age is not a criterion for miracles; they happen at all ages. But perhaps we have been too quick to call them "lucky breaks." We notice all miracles, be they large or small, only when we reach the stage of being open to the possibility of their occurring. William Barry, S.J., emphasizes the necessity of approaching everything and everyone as part of God's creation and worthy of our respect, no matter what the circumstances. He writes, "To be a contemplative in action is to contemplate (or find) God in our daily lives, in our activity. If we were contemplatives in action, we would approach everyone and everything with reverence."[9]

For those who wish to repeat Peter's inspired action, I must stress that many of the poor on the streets have physical or psychiatric disabilities of a serious nature. These handicaps cannot be ignored. It is difficult to differentiate those who are down because of unforeseen circumstances from those who have medical problems requiring medical and/or psychiatric treatment. The latter often require several team members from various specialties acting in concert. Nevertheless, a prayer can be a blessing to persons in either circumstance.

You Are as Old as You Feel

Age can be a matter of one's mental attitude toward life. During the Hungarian Revolution (1955–56), I was assigned to a navy ship (as ship's medical officer) responsible for transporting 2,500 men, women, and children each trip from Bremerhaven, Germany, to New York. All these individuals had escaped from the Iron Curtain nations of Latvia, Estonia, Lithuania, East Germany, Poland, Hungary, Czechoslovakia, and Yugoslavia to the freedom of Western Europe. After completing twelve round trips across the bumpy North Atlantic, it occurred to me that I had been responsible for the health of some 30,000 of these prospective American citizens. I collected and saved a number of anecdotes during that stint of duty, ranging from death-defying escapes to humorous incidents. One of the passengers was a sixty-five-year-old farmer from Yugoslavia going to his new home in Oregon who couldn't wait "to get started in farming all over again!" Yet how many times do we physicians see forty- and fifty-year-old patients with minor complaints describing how "terrible it is to get older." They predict the bronchitis that "always hits the last week in September every year" and sure enough, they are correct!

Our negative attitudes seem to play an important role in causation of illness. One explanation for this relationship is that anxiety and negative thoughts decrease the effectiveness of the immune mechanism, that is, decrease our ability to resist illness. It has been shown that "killer T-cells," which fight infections and cancer, are decreased when one is full of anxiety, and the opposite occurs when one is upbeat and optimistic about the outcome of the illness.[10]

This relationship was demonstrated by a group of investigators in Florida in the early 1980s, whose work led to the formation of the American Academy of Psychoimmunology.[11] Who would have thought that those interested in scientific research and biochemistry (the immunologists) would team up with psychologists dealing with emotions and human behavior? But how one thinks has much to do with healing. Trusting God in all things and conditions creates an inner peace, the effect of which research is beginning to reveal in the form of an enhanced immune system.

Further Reading

Ader, Robert, David L. Felten, and Nicholas Cohen, *Psychoneuroimmunology,* 2nd ed. (San Diego: Academic Press, 1991).

This book outlines the growing literature on the interconnection between the nervous system, endocrine system, and immune system and how emotional states affect an individual's health and immune response.

William A. Barry, S.J., *Finding God in All Things: A Companion to the Spiritual Exercises of St. Ignatius* (Notre Dame, Ind.: Ave Maria Press, 1991).

The basis for this special book is connecting Ignatian spirituality to modern living, a mission that is accomplished well by Reverend Barry. He helps us realize that being a contemplative is not only desirable but is God's will for each of us. By daily meditation, we quietly listen, pray, and reflect upon God's word. Father Barry then leads us from daily meditation to seeing God in all things, in essence becoming "contemplatives in action."

7

Tobacco and Cardiovascular Disease

B ecause smoking is such a serious risk factor in the field of cardiovascular disease, a few statistics appear warranted whenever one is discussing the upkeep and maintenance of the body temple. About 565,000 people die from coronary artery disease in the United States each year, and about 30 percent of these deaths are attributable to smoking.[1] Thirty percent of all cancer deaths are attributable to smoking, that is, about 125,000 of 412,000 deaths annually (80 percent of these deaths are from lung cancer). These statistics do not include deaths due to other diseases strongly attributed to smoking, such as chronic bronchitis and emphysema. All this adds up to health-care costs of $16 billion per year due to lost earnings, disability payments, and smoking-related fires. Dr. Jonathan Fielding, writing in the *New England Journal of Medicine*, noted that men between the ages of forty and fifty-nine years of age who smoked one or more packs of cigarettes daily had a 2.5 times greater risk of serious heart condition than nonsmokers. An article published in the *Journal of the American Medical Association,* in December 1991, noted that more than 1 million Americans become new smokers each year, most of these children and adolescents. Since 80 percent of all adult smokers become regular smokers before their twenty-first birthday, it is even more crucial that young people be prevented from starting. Although 42 million

Americans have stopped smoking, 28 percent of the population continue to smoke.[2]

The good news is that the risk for premature heart disease decreases almost 50 percent upon cessation of smoking. However, it may be another ten years before one reaches the same risk level as one's nonsmoking counterpart. Pipe smokers and cigar smokers fall between nonsmokers and cigarette smokers as far as risk factors for coronary artery disease.

Smokers seem to age faster in other ways too—more wrinkles, poorer endurance and lung capacity, and often more respiratory infections.

The Smoking Teenager

I was part of a research team that conducted a study of 191 male students ages fourteen to nineteen in 1966, when smoking among males in this age group was perhaps a bit more common than today. Heavy smokers (those who smoked ten or more cigarettes a day) had 6.5 times more lower respiratory infections and 2.6 times more upper respiratory infections than nonsmokers.

We found that identification with fellow students and with older friends who smoked were the most influential factors encouraging the smoking habit. On the other hand, participation in competitive sports was considered most important in discouraging smoking. Although not significant enough to warrant statistics, a trend emerged, even at this young age, toward diminished lung capacity among the smoking students.[3]

A study performed by a group of doctors at L.S.U. Medical Center New Orleans in 1989, the Bogalusa Heart Study, examined a large group of children, noting which risk factors during the first two decades of life contributed to adult heart disease.[4] This study confirmed the belief that adult hypertension as well as coronary artery disease have their roots in childhood. For example, the study found that children of white men who had heart attacks were more likely to smoke cigarettes and be obese than children whose fathers had no history of heart attacks. This finding could be attributed to the children's mimicking of their fathers' behaviors. After twenty years of following 14,000 individuals from Bogalusa, Louisiana, data indicate that cardiac risk factors can be identified in young children, that atherosclerosis (deposits in the coronary arteries) can begin as early as three years of age, that risk factors remain stable over time, and that behavior that affects risk factors is learned early in life.

Thus, it is crucial to their future well-being that we educate children about heart health in the home, in school, on the street, and even through television. Such messages could depict the grim reality of patients with severe heart disease— taking oxygen at home, being weak and short of breath, and having a decreased appetite. Several of my patients who were dying from heart disease, emphysema, cirrhosis of the liver, or other diseases caused largely by poor lifestyle choices agreed to be subjects for a videotape depicting their current poor state of health if it would help deter young people from following a similar path. I've always thought that peer pressure, meeting actual people with a given disease, and the health habits of parents have more of an impact upon children than reading material or lectures. Further, it always made more sense to me to show an anti-smoking "commercial," featuring a live but very sick patient (with his or her consent, of course), when millions of viewers are watching than to distribute printed material that may reach only a handful of children. Such a "commercial" was aired on TV in the mid-1980s—actor Yul Brynner made public service announcements when he was dying of lung cancer. He said in the spots that he might be dead by the time it was aired. And indeed he was. (He died on October 10, 1985.) It was quite chilling and sent a strong message against smoking. Schools could be given copies of these "commercials," and teachers could discuss them with their students. Similarly, schools could arrange for a physician or nurse to discuss tobacco use and bodily damage.

Encouraging teenagers to do aerobic activities, regardless of their skills or coordination (simpler and/or noncompetitive activities can be devised for those who are not interested in sports or who are physically challenged), reinforces good health habits. Those who have a natural affinity for sports learn that the stopwatch will soon weed out the smoker from the nonsmoker. It's been my experience that very few youngsters who run track or swim competitively subsequently take up smoking as adults. This is important since most smoking adults started the habit as teenagers. Parents must encourage their children to participate in athletics wherever possible by attending games, driving them to and from drills, practicing with them at home, and supporting them even when they don't win. Parents usually enjoy meeting other parents who encourage their children to take part in athletics. Friendships between two generations can develop that will likely last beyond high school or college. This happened with my two sons and daughter. They never smoked; they were involved in competitive sports throughout their school years; and by God's grace they continue to work out on a regular basis and enjoy excellent health. Despite the realization that there is more to healthy living than just good genes and the absence of major accidents or catastrophic illnesses, there are still those who fail to care for the body temple and, hence, suffer needlessly.

The Smoker Who Never Quit

Harry, a seventy-seven-year-old retired mail clerk, had been a heavy cigarette smoker most of his life and consequently suffered from pulmonary emphysema and chronic bronchitis for a good portion of it. In his later years, he was connected to an oxygen tank equipped with a long leash that enabled him to walk around his room at home. On more than one occasion, he disconnected himself from the oxygen machine long enough to smoke a cigarette. When off the oxygen, his lips turned blue. After finishing his cigarette, he would cough for several moments and would then immediately reattach the oxygen. Harry died from pneumonia complicated by a severe case of emphysema. I wonder if Harry had a subconscious death wish.

Typically, two types of patients can stop smoking fairly easily. One is the individual in the coronary care unit just admitted with a heart attack; the other has just been shown a chest X-ray revealing a well-defined cancer of the lung. In both cases there is a remarkable loss of desire to smoke as well as an absence of withdrawal symptoms—both are frightened out of their wits. With the necessary support and a chorus of "You have no choice!" ringing in their ears, these patients rarely start smoking again (more of this later).

One of the greatest joys for a practicing cardiologist is to see a positive change in a patient's health. Let's say a doctor examines a patient, who has been taking a host of medications for palpitations. After encouraging the patient to adopt a healthier lifestyle, the patient does so and returns with virtually no palpitations and with no further need for prescription drugs. Obviously, this improvement is not always possible. But by stopping all tobacco, caffeine, and alcohol intake, by getting more rest, by setting aside a quiet time during the day, by watching one's diet, and by exercising regularly to relieve stress—in other words, by "working with nature"—it is possible to both ameliorate the palpitations and help transform the entire body temple. Patients appreciate this approach and are invariably proud of themselves for accomplishing so much "on their own." They like themselves better, they feel better, they enjoy doing aerobic exercise, and they especially appreciate the dramatic drop in expensive drug prescriptions.

It takes a multidimensional approach to persuade people to stop smoking. Cigar, cigarette, and pipe smoke can be absorbed through the mucous membranes of the mouth, in a manner not unlike the way medicine in a rectal suppository is absorbed. Thus, no one is really free from tobacco's ills, even those who rationalize their habit by insisting that they don't inhale. What's more, passive smoke can be harmful to non-smokers who inhale smoke from nearby tobacco users.

The nicotine patch, along with follow-up support by the office nurse and active interest and participation by the family physician, has been the most successful way to kick the habit. Each visit, the physician explains, exhorts, and praises the patient with his or her struggle. The chewing gum Nicorettes can also help, but nurse-physician encouragement is the best motivator and should be employed as much as possible.

Over the years, patients have tried biofeedback, hypnosis, group sessions, medications, public lectures, acupuncture, and even waging bets to stop smoking without any consistent success. Taking up wind-building sports, such as squash or jogging has more positive effects. At some point the individual realizes that it is counterproductive to build endurance while continuing to smoke. It is also helpful to list the specific bio-chemical or physiological reasons (such as emphysema, coronary artery disease, or poor circulation) why it is important for the patient to stop immediately. Dealing in specifics rather than generalities is preferred. Most patients are receptive and understand simple terminology and can relate it to their individual situation quite easily.

Despite our great concerns about rising health-care costs, many people still say, "Insurance will pay for it." This, of course, means an increase in the yearly premiums for everyone, including the individual making the statement. For a moment, pretend that you don't have adequate health insurance and that you must pay out of your pocket $10,000 for an illness that may have been prevented by following a better lifestyle. If that were the case, I wonder how many of us would be more willing to make the appropriate lifestyle changes, including the elimination of tobacco?

The American Heart Association estimates that there are about 2.2 million teenage smokers in the U.S. between the ages of twelve and seventeen according to a report that appeared in the *Journal of the American Medical Association* in 1993. The same report indicated that as many as 3,000 teenagers start to smoke every day in this country.[5] Surgeon General M. Joycelyn Elders claims that smoking poses a significant health hazard to the very young, as an estimated 9 million children in the U.S., younger than five years, live with at least one smoker.[6] These children are exposed regularly to second-hand smoke.

It has been known for some time that maternal smoking during pregnancy is associated with low birth weight of infants, infant deaths, and long-term neurotoxicity, which causes behavior disorders. But recently new evidence reported by Dr. Gideon Koren from the Hospital for Sick Children in Toronto revealed that infants of smokers had significant amounts of nicotine in hair samples. Even infants born to mothers who were passive smokers had significant amounts of nicotine in the neonatal hair, although this group was about one-quarter the size of the group of infants born to smoking mothers who had significant amounts of nicotine in the neonatal hair.[7]

Each state has its own laws regarding the sale of cigarettes and tobacco to minors. In New Jersey, for example, those selling or giving cigarettes to minors (children under age eighteen) are fined $250. The state legislature is now voting on a bevy of bills to prohibit smoking in all restaurants and public places, to forbid sale of single cigarettes, and to prohibit cigarette advertising within 1,000 feet of a school.

There is increasing legislative interest in restricting the sale of tobacco to children in the same way that the sale of alcohol is restricted. The logical extension of this would be to ban all tobacco ads in magazines and on billboards (cigarette ads were banned from television in the 1970s) and prohibiting the distribution of free samples.

Smoking after a Heart Attack

I've had only a handful of patients who smoked after recovering from a heart attack. John, a sixty-five-year-old professor from one of the local universities, was my first patient to do so. I reminded him that smoking after a heart attack was the greatest single factor contributing to a second attack. He said he realized it was serious, but he was in the middle of a scientific breakthrough, was delivering many lectures, writing papers, and doing a lot of traveling. This was not the best time to stop, he insisted. John died at the prime of his career, while leading a panel discussion, with a cigarette, literally, in his mouth.

The second patient I had who continued to smoke was a forty-two-year-old used car dealer, Henry. He would stop for a few days and then start up again. He also suffered a second attack but, fortunately, he survived. He finally accepted the admonition that he "had no choice" and never smoked again.

The third individual was a writer, Walter, age sixty, who had recently recovered from a heart attack. One day, during a routine follow-up visit, I was dismayed to learn he was still smoking. I turned to him toward the end of the visit and said, "I've only had three patients smoke after a heart attack, the professor who died, the car dealer who had his second one but lived, and now (pointing my finger at him) YOU!" He was so shocked and scared that he threw the pack of cigarettes into the wastebasket and never smoked again. Such straightforwardness, as well as firmly stating that the individual has no choice but to quit, has persuaded the overwhelming majority of my heart attack patients to never smoke again.

Dr. Harvey D. White, a physician from New Zealand, and his colleagues studied 456 acute myocardial infarction patients and followed their progress for one year. This 1991 study confirms prior data that indicated that smoking after a heart attack can have very serious consequences. The study found that patients who continued to smoke after a heart attack were 20 percent more likely to suffer a second heart attack compared to the 5.1 percent for those who had stopped completely.[8]

One weekend in 1960, while I was a senior resident in medicine, I had the responsibility for all medical admissions to the private practice wing of a large New York City hospital. From Friday evening to Monday morning, I saw many patients admitted for various conditions. But what struck me most was the ages of three male patients admitted for heart attacks—all three younger than I. The first man was a twenty-eight-year-old graduate student who died; the second a thirty-one-year-old FBI agent having his second heart attack; the third was a thirty-year-old businessman. The latter two survived. All three were heavy cigarette smokers. Since then, whenever I see a new patient who is young and male and a smoker, I routinely order an electrocardiogram (EKG) as a precaution.

Smoking can cause other adverse cardiovascular effects. Smoking can allow blood platelets to become more sticky and likely to lead to thrombosis (clotting) of vessels. The nicotine can also cause spasms of the arteries, leading to very poor circulation in the lower extremities.

The Plumber with Blue Feet

Jerry, a forty-one-year-old plumber, came to the office complaining that his feet had become cold and blue since he had started to smoke (which was only a few weeks earlier). His feet indeed were cold and the pulse was mostly gone, much different from prior examinations over the years. Needless to say it did not take much argument to convince him to stop smoking immediately as he was sure both legs would soon fall off. After he stopped smoking for one week, his feet returned to their warm, pink color once again.

This case is a poignant example of how smoking can cause constriction of the arteries to the lower extremities. Cigarette smoking is a major factor in developing poor circulation in the legs. In fact, 98 percent of patients with severe narrowing of the large vessels to the legs have a significant smoking history. Smokers have at least a two to three times greater chance of dying from a dilated portion of the aorta in the abdomen (abdominal aortic aneurysm) than nonsmokers.[9] Nicotine has also been implicated in causing arrhythmias (disturbances of heart rhythm); it can raise the cholesterol and lower the HDL; and it lowers the amount of oxygen transported from the lungs to the body tissues. Some evidence suggests that inhaled smoke (whether firsthand or secondhand) decreases the amount of oxygen attached to the hemoglobin molecule, which is needed to supply the body tissues. Instead the molecule is partially replaced with carboxyhemoglobin, which is thought to be one of the agents that can cause cholesterol to form in the lumens of the coronary arteries and which can eventually lead to narrowing and blockage, culminating in coronary thrombosis or heart attack.

More recently there has been a surge of interest in the potential damage smoking has on nonsmokers living with smokers. One study revealed that the risk for lung cancer of a nonsmoking spouse of a heavy smoker was 3.5 times greater than the risk of a spouse of a nonsmoker.[10] Other researchers have also found a trend toward greater incidence of lung cancer in the nonsmoking spouse. Lung cancer causes the death of approximately 3,000 never-smokers every year as the result of exposure to environmental tobacco.[11] The public health hazard of passive inhalation of tobacco smoke is thought to increase the risk of heart disease more than the risk of lung cancer. Other symptoms experienced by passive smokers—that is, nonsmokers who inhale the smoke of nearby smokers—include eye irritation, nasal congestion, allergic attacks, and angina (chest pain) occurring at low levels of exercise.

Not surprisingly, asthmatic children of smoking parents improve when both parents stop smoking. Infants born to mothers who smoked during pregnancy were born with lower birth weights than infants of nonsmoking mothers.

Smokers also appear to have a greater risk of strokes. In one study women smokers who used the birth control pill were found to be 21.9 times more at risk of stroke than nonsmoking women. Ample studies already link cancer of the larynx, oral cancer, carcinoma of the esophagus, cancer of the bladder, and cancer of the pancreas with tobacco use. Chronic obstructive lung disease (pulmonary emphysema) is about thirty times more common in smokers than in nonsmokers. Likewise, there is a higher incidence of peptic ulcer in smokers (two times higher in male smokers and almost as much in female smokers).Very recent studies now suggest a linkage between cigarette smoking and cataract formation. Perhaps as many as 20 percent of patients can attribute their cataracts to smoking.[12]

The enormous personal, social, and economic cost that could be eliminated or greatly reduced by ending society's tobacco use is nothing short of mind-boggling! We must remember that the real cause for celebration in this arena is not the successful heart or lung transplant (as nice as this may be for a given patient), but the fact that thousands have stopped smoking or never started in the first place.

Unfortunately, the tobacco industry does not share our desire for celebration. Tobacco companies still deny real linkage between smoking and health problems, and the tobacco lobby has enormous influence in Washington. The industry's great financial interest in keeping people smoking and enticing new people to smoke has made it and continues to make it difficult to stop this health- and life-threatening habit.

Further Reading

Jonathan Fielding, "Smoking: Health Effects and Control," *New England Journal of Medicine* 313, no. 8 (1985): 491–97.

Fielding's review of the health dangers of tobacco is one of the best I've read. It encompasses the entire spectrum of tobacco-induced illnesses brought on up smoking. The vast number of organ systems injured by tobacco is a revelation. The study remains a potent argument against tobacco and its major role in slowly destroying the body temple.

8

Stress and Retirement

A t some point in time we must all face the emotional chal-
lenge of retirement. Whether it is because of age, illness,
or loss of job the time to retire will arrive. One frequently
heard complaint from wives after their husband's retirement
is, "Ever since George has retired, he tells me how to run the
house, cook, and clean, and is generally under foot every time
I turn around." After we retire we need to find new interests
or expand old ones to take the place of our work. Otherwise
we are liable to drive ourselves (and our spouses) up a wall.

By and large, most of my patients who have retired do not
miss getting up and going through the hassles that were so
common during their preretirement years. One study about
the stress of retirement upon 1,516 male participants revealed
that, for those retired less than a year, retirement was not as
traumatic an event as they expected. However, 30 percent of
those retired for *more* than a year did find it stressful. Then
again, twice as many actively employed (65 percent) found
working a stressful condition.[1] Health and financial problems
were the most influential factors in affecting the stress levels
of the retirees. Subjects whose retirement was recent (less
than a year), found that out of thirty-one life stresses (such as
death of a child or spouse, divorce, major health problem,
and financial loss) retirement was ranked number thirty-one.[2]

In his book *The Stress of Life*, Hans Selye states that,
because aging does not progress at the same speed in everyone, many capable people have been forced to leave the job

market when they reached an arbitrarily set age. This situation results in what he calls *retirement disease.* Individuals may become physically ill and prematurely senile when forced to retire when they are still active and creative.[3]

Upon the completion of twenty-five to thirty years of work for a particular business, the retiree often has high expectations for his or her last day on the job—if not the local high school band waiting to play in his or her honor, at least some sort of big fuss to reward years of faithful service. However, such a display does not often occur in the real world.

> I retired about a year ago after twenty-five years as Director of Laundry and Linen Services and my last day on the job was very uneventful. I said good-bye to a few department heads with whom I was very friendly and my administrator, had lunch with my assistant manager and left. There was no fanfare announcing my departure.[4]

Very often our sense of dedication to work and our integrity are award enough even the hoopla will be forgotten in a short while. We hope that the friendships will continue and the good times will be remembered.

I have observed that volunteer work of some kind or beginning a new activity such as painting results in a better sense of self-worth after retirement. Nevertheless, many experience retirement, the end of their career, whether it is forced or expected, as a great loss that must be grieved. Our society teaches us that we must achieve to be successful. But society has not taught us how to lose gracefully, whether it is our health, our vocation, our roots, or our relationships that we are losing. We often forget that sudden and unexpected changes in our lives can be cause for grief. We feel that we have lost something dear, and so we mourn. John W. James and Frank Cherry, in *The Grief Recovery Handbook,* write, "My happiness depends on the choice within me to not fight with changes beyond my control. My happiness depends on my willingness to accept these changes." They go on to say:

> It's so simple. Like having a rose garden. It is impossible to have a rose garden and not experience pain and joy in working with it. . . . It takes more than time to clean up a

rose garden. It takes willingness and acceptance to do the work. With these things, it takes much less time than I originally thought. To feel better in such a short amount of time is grace. It seems like so much work until I get started. Only then do the results become a reality.[5]

A Retirement Necessitated by Disability

One of my patients, Rob, was forced to retire from the clothing store at which he had worked for years because of a progressive neurological condition, A.L.S. (amyotrophic lateral sclerosis, also known as Lou Gehrig's disease.) For the past several years, he has worked five days a week at a local physical rehabilitation center as a volunteer. He is well liked and has always tried to help those in the rehabilitation program. As his own condition slowly deteriorated, he found walking more and more difficult. When Rob first started his volunteer work, he was able to get around with the aid of a cane. He always visited with the patients and tried to encourage them, asking, "Can I help you? I am a volunteer here to help you in any way possible." With the passage of time and the slow progress of his disease, Rob eventually had to resort to crutches. Again, he offered his help as a volunteer, frequently stating that he was a good listener if there was anything on their minds that they wanted to talk about or that he could write a letter for them if they wished. As more time passed, his condition reached the point where he had to rely on a wheelchair to get about. Still he asks, as he wheels himself into the recreation area wearing his blue volunteer jacket, "Can I help you?" What a source of inspiration and what a powerful message he brings to others! His reaching out to others, the majority of whom are far less disabled, has served as a powerful ministry and a source of encouragement to all connected with the center—patients and staff alike. But Rob has received a blessing as well. It has given him a purpose to keep living and a sense of worth no amount of money could buy. As the physical component of his body temple has slowly disintegrated, the spiritual component has expanded. His message has become stronger. By allowing himself to be a channel of caring and encouragement to others, the Lord has given Rob an inner peace and sense of purpose that has enabled him to accept his own general physical deterioration. Rob's neurological condition progressed unusually slowly, and I wonder whether this especially is part of God's plan for him. It has been twenty years since the diagnosis was first made. I am certain the Lord is using him as a channel of healing and grace for others.

The following words of Paul speak to Rob's example.

Therefore, my beloved, be steadfast, immovable, always excelling in the work of the Lord, because you know that in the Lord your labor is not in vain.

–1 Corinthians 15:58

The reaction of the new retiree to his or her new status can vary depending on the circumstances under which the retirement took place. For example, an early retirement resulting from job loss can be very disquieting. On the other hand, a long-awaited retirement, happily executed, is a different kettle of fish. The loss of a job due to a serious illness or injury also has a different impact on retirement activities, trips, and one's general sense of wellness.

Under most circumstances retirement is a time of transition and adjustments—retiring "from" one stage of life "to" another—a time of re-creation and recreation, of opening up new opportunities for growth. This period may be difficult, but with counseling, support groups of other retirees, and family emotional help, the transition can be made.

A Life of Service

Muriel is my maiden aunt whose retirement was planned and focused around being of service. She was a member of the U.S. Navy Waves during World War II, then worked at Fort Monmouth, New Jersey, Army Signal Corps as a civil service employee for about thirty years, after which she retired with a government pension. Being always independent and self-sufficient, she joined the Peace Corps and spent two years in Peru at age sixty teaching farmers how to keep better records. (She had an accounting background.) While there, she lived in a hut, slept on a dirt floor, and did not seem to miss the many niceties found back home. After the two years were over, she volunteered for Vista and worked with Native Americans in the hills outside Salt Lake City, serving as a volunteer social worker. These families were living in poverty and required proper housing, clothes, and medical care. Then, after moving back East, she helped Spanish-speaking migrant farmers with their tax forms and record-keeping for a few years, Spanish having become a second language by this time. After she moved to a retirement village, she spent time with Meals on Wheels, delivering food to the needy in the area. Recently, however, at the age of eighty, she had to stop because she felt her vision no longer permitted her to drive safely. Though she is a low-key and soft-spoken individual, she stands as a role model for all of us, being of service to others in her own quiet way. Muriel retired from the Signal Corps, but she did not retire from life. She continued to be active and gained great personal satisfaction by using her unique gifts to help others.

The Effects of Unrelieved Stress

Brendon was a highly specialized engineer in the aerospace industry. With the cut back of government funds, he, along with many co-workers, found himself without a job at age forty-five. Now he works part-time taking tickets at movie theaters and as a cashier at a supermarket while he attends night school to learn more about computer science. Brendon had no time to formulate a game plan for his retirement.

Dr. Robert S. Eliot studied the effects of sudden job disruption upon workers in similar vocations at the Kennedy Space Center several years ago. He found, not unexpectedly, that such stress was associated with a larger number of heart attacks than would normally be expected in this age group, as well as a higher incidence of alcoholism and divorce.[6] Excess cortisone is produced by constant stress (such as that caused by unhappy work environment, life changes, or family problems). This process is quite different from the "fight-or-flight" reflex in which adrenaline is produced. Unlike our prehistoric ancestors we cannot kill or escape from our bosses when we are faced with stress at work. Unrelieved stress can result in the production of enough excess cortisone to cause intestinal bleeding, heart attacks, and other serious medical problems. Stress must be dealt with or the whole body temple suffers.

Forced Retirement and the Search for Inner Peace

Harry is a patient of mine and a research chemist. He was very upset when, after working twenty years for a large pharmaceutical company, he was let go as part of a "downsizing" program (which we read about so frequently these days). I remember him saying, when the forced retirement occurred, that he found the job boring, hated to get up in the morning knowing that although he had to face another day at work, and just couldn't wait until he had a few more years into a pension plan so that he could retire, this retirement had happened much sooner than he desired! Fortunately, he soon found another position in a smaller company, working as a biochemist. He loves the work and the staff, and he now has a sizable crew working under his supervision. When I ask him how his work is going, he chuckles and has said more than once, "The best thing that ever happened was to be shoved into early retirement; I really hated that old job."

The stories are endless but by and large most of the retired patients I know are enjoying their lives, traveling, auditing classes, volunteering, and keeping active both mentally and physically.

Inner peace has a salutary effect upon the immune mechanism, while a chaotic state of mind often produces the opposite result. As stress caused by the transition of retirement or other factors is and will be with all of us while we make our earthly journey, it is important to cultivate a healthy lifestyle early in life and to maintain it for the rest of our lives. Such a lifestyle includes proper rest, good diet, exercise, and avoiding drugs, alcohol, and tobacco. Researchers have found a direct relationship between stress and a reduced immune response.[7] The inner peace achieved by recognizing God's presence in all things is also a strong factor in dealing with stress and thus in helping the immune system. We must realize that each of us is loved by our Lord. He has a perfect plan for each of us, but we must be tuned in to his presence—the kingdom of God that is within us. He calls us and beckons to us constantly, but we are often too busy to listen. We need his spiritual nourishment for our wholeness.

9

Exercise and the Aging Body Temple

R egular exercise has been amply shown to modify the aging process in all age groups, but most noticeably among those in the middle and later years of life. This is a time of life when we all look around for the "fountain of youth" as we find ourselves slowing down and discover more than a few creaking joints. Some researchers are saying that daily exercise is indeed the treasure that has been sought over time, and I must agree with that point of view. This is why I feel it is imperative for teenagers to begin a healthy lifestyle early.

Physical Benefits of Regular Exercise

Regular exercise is a strong factor in attaining a satisfactory body weight, blowing off tensions, improving blood cholesterol level and the levels of other blood lipids, and reducing blood pressure and pulse rate (allowing the heart to do its work with less effort), and it is also an opportunity to enjoy the company of others participating in the same activity. Further, it makes the blood platelets less sticky (less likely to clog up the arteries and cause a thrombosis) and delays bone thinning (osteoporosis). It has been suggested that exercise can avert diabetes by reducing blood sugar and making body cells more sensitive to insulin.[1] Those who exercise regularly are, in general, better tuned in to good health habits.

Companies such as Johnson and Johnson in New Jersey make time for exercise breaks.[2] An unusual incentive by one company (Atco Properties and Management in Manhattan) is to offer pay incentives and other benefits to employees who daily walk up the sixteen flights to the office for one year instead of taking the elevator. Other companies offer financial rewards for the cessation of smoking, losing excess weight, or, in the case of Mesa Limited Partnership in Dallas, $354 extra each year for every employee who exercises at least thirteen times per month. It has been their experience that the fit worker is a healthier one with less absenteeism and more efficient work, resulting in savings for the company.

One is never too old to start exercise, but the exercise we choose should be enjoyable and within our physical abilities. People often need encouragement from peers as well as their physician to exercise regularly. Of course, before one begins a new exercise regimen, one's family doctor should perform a physical exam, laboratory tests, and other necessary tests (such as stress tests or echocardiograms). After my patients have been cleared medically to undertake an exercise program, I tell them, "Exercise so that you are pleasantly out of breath." Moderate regular exercise, preferably six or seven days a week for about one half hour or more is appropriate for the middle aged and the elderly.

Only 27 percent of those over sixty-five in this country exercise regularly.[3] As the years fly by in the middle and later years, maintaining flexibility, muscle strength, and stamina are all necessary for good body function and independent living, enabling one to be less dependent on others for routine activities. I hope to illustrate examples of individuals who have been able to delay the aging process in various ways through adhering to an exercise program.

Bone loss (osteoporosis) starts in women by the age of thirty-five and by the age of fifty-five among men.[4] Weight-bearing exercises (such as walking and running) are beneficial and increase the mineral content and density of the bones. The large numbers of hip fractures that the elderly suffer following falls is related to bone thinning.

Exercise is necessary for every adult. However, the following conditions should be kept in mind. Extreme temperatures (hot or cold) should be avoided. Exercise should not be undertaken until one or two hours after a meal. Exercisers should warm-up for at least five minutes (stretching and walking) before beginning their routine and should cool down for at least five minutes afterward. If one has been away from regular exercise for several days, it is better to restart at a lower level of intensity. The arms can tax the heart more than the legs. I've often told my elderly patients, especially my heart patients, that it would be better for them to walk a few miles than to strain trying to raise a window that is stuck or lift a heavy load of fertilizer. Adequate footwear should be used for walking or jogging. Make sure that they are comfortable and have enough spring in the soles to protect the joints in the feet, knees, and low back (I suggest using running shoes). I discourage scuba diving for the elderly and also exercising at high altitudes (above 10,000 feet). On days of high air pollution, it is better not to exercise outdoors.

For all age groups, regular exercise leads to a better self-image, a sense of well-being, improved sleep patterns, less depression, and an improved immune system. All of us who have been in the practice of medicine for any length of time have noted that patients who exercise regularly have shorter recovery times from operations and illnesses. They seem to have a better resistance to disease, exemplified by fewer respiratory infections. Researchers recently reported in the *British Journal of Cancer* a lower prevalence of breast cancer and cancer of the reproductive system among former college athletes compared to nonathletes.[5] It has been suggested that regular exercise can lead to the endurance, flexibility, and strength equal in many cases to that of a nonexercising individual twenty years younger.[6]

Exercise also may attenuate some of the side effects of pregnancy, such as varicose veins, fluid retention, backache, elevated blood pressure, and excessive weight gain. Workers in the field of sports physiology feel that it takes about two weeks of maintaining a conditioning program before an effect can be noted. Unfortunately, deconditioning starts as soon as one stops the program, and it has been said that one becomes almost totally deconditioned, a novice starting all over again, following three weeks without training. There appears to be a healthy "addiction" to daily exercise so that, when even a few days pass without exercise, a person will complain of feeling out of sorts, tired, and listless. Then the individual realizes the cause of the problem, "No wonder I feel so bad; I haven't done any exercise for the past three or four days." The body temple is reminding the person to get back into the swing of things. Occasionally it may be necessary to rest the body or switch from activities if the body is complaining too much (having sore knees or hip pain, for example). Fifteen years ago I switched from jogging to the swimming pool as I was experiencing joint pain in my legs. However, Dr. Nancy E. Lane and co-workers, writing in the *American Journal of Medicine* in 1987 found that members of a running club (averaging about sixty years of age) had less overall physical disabilities than age-matched controls who did not exercise regularly. Runners demonstrated better cardiovascular fitness, weighed less, and had surprisingly fewer upper and lower extremity musculoskeletal disabilities than the age-matched nonexercising controls. In addition, the runners were overall more free of illness, missed less work, and felt better than the control group.[7]

There is ample research documenting the decline in one's fitness as one ages. You have only to reflect on this for a moment to know that this pertains not only to yourself but also to your friends. However, by exercising a large number of people seem to be doing a better job of holding back Father Time than the majority of their contemporaries.

Age and Exercise Capacity

One measure of fitness is called the maximum oxygen uptake. This measurement, along with measurements dealing with body strength and speed, have been shown to drop by 1 percent per year starting at age twenty-five in sedentary people. Many researchers feel this 1 percent loss of fitness per year most likely applies to the sedentary lifestyle rather than to age alone.[8] Dr. Phil Whitten has been studying a group of Masters swimmers of various ages for the past fifteen years (and intends to continue the study for many years to come). Approximately 25,000 men and women swimmers ranging in age from late teens to octogenarians, sometimes older, are registered members of the U.S. Masters Swimming Association. Many compete in meets for their age divisions (each division is five years apart) at the national, local, and international level. Records of the top ten in all age brackets are kept for each year for the four basic strokes as well as for relays. Whitten found that for swimmers in their early forties the rate of decline in fitness was .13 percent per year, or one eighth that of the sedentary controls. He noted that swimmers don't reach the 1 percent per year decline until their early seventies. His work suggests that a sedentary person has a 25 percent loss of fitness when he or she reaches fifty years of age; by contrast, the active swimmer by age fifty has only a 3.5 percent loss of fitness![9]

It has been shown that, from age twenty to seventy, muscle mass decreases by about 30 percent and the metabolism reduces 2 percent every ten years. This means that we need fewer calories each day as we age unless we increase our exercise. Therefore, if we exercise regularly, we may not have to significantly cut calorie intake to avoid weight gain. As our population ages, the following seems especially pertinent:

> Strengthen the weak hands,
> and make firm the feeble knees.
>
> Say to those who are of a fearful heart,
> "Be strong, do not fear!
>
> Here is your God.
> He will come with vengeance,
> with terrible recompense.
> He will come and save you."
>
> Then the eyes of the blind shall be opened,
> and the ears of the deaf unstopped;
> then the lame shall leap like a deer,
> and the tongue of the speechless sing for joy.
> –Isaiah 35:3–6

Fitness Studies among the Elderly

It is generally accepted among sports physiologists that improved exercise capacity can be proportionally as great in older people as in younger ones. It is never too late to start a supervised training program. A 1990 article in the *Journal of Sports Medicine and Physical Fitness* by a group of exercise physiologists reports the findings of a four-month study on twenty-eight healthy, sedentary men and women aged fifty-five to seventy. One group exercised actively (brisk walking), the other did stretching and flexibility exercises only. Both groups improved at the end of the study, the actively exercising group doing slightly better. It seems that even relatively mild exercise such as stretching can bring about improvement.[10]

Dr. Paul Hutinger is both an exercise physiologist and a world-class swimmer with a number of national records to his credit. This is double trouble for me as I usually swim in the U.S. National Championships (U.S. Masters) every year, as he does, and we are in the same age group. You can guess who the winner is in my heat! Nevertheless, as one "ages up," that is, moves into different age groups (I've been swimming in the Masters since 1973), improving one's time in an event is as exciting as placing or winning. As mentioned above, the average rate of decline of exercise capacity is about 1 percent per year after one's mid-twenties. Between 1971 and 1986 (ages forty-six to sixty-two), Hutinger's exercise capacity fell off an average of only 1 percent every five years instead of the expected 1 percent per year.

On a more modest scale, I was thrilled to have the best times in the 50-meter and 100-meter backstroke at a meet in 1993, bettering a time set in 1977 in the former event and 1973 in the latter. I must have made a lucky turn at the end of the pool that day.*

Ashby Harper, of the class of '39 at Princeton University, was, at sixty-five, the oldest person to swim the English Channel. In 1990, he swam around Manhattan Island for the

---

* Editor's note: The writer has been in the top ten in the U.S. Masters Swimming Association in backstroke every year for the past several years.

third time; the most recent attempt was faster than his first trip in 1983. Ashby's case further exemplifies the benefits of regular exercise, even if it's begun when one is older.

Drs. William Evans and Irwin Rosenberg of the Human Nutrition Research Center on Aging at Tufts University noted instances of men in their mid-seventies who were able to improve their lifting power from 44 pounds to 85 pounds and concomitantly lose fat and gain muscle during a three-month period. Likewise, women in their nineties tripled their strength in a period of eight weeks. All of this was done through supervised weight training.[11]

In another attempt to study the effect of aerobic exercise upon fitness, low-impact (one foot in contact with the floor at all times) aerobic dance routine was studied using sixty-five women volunteers ages fifty-five to seventy-seven years (mean age sixty-five). Researchers randomly assigned thirty-five women to the exercise group and thirty to the control group, which carried on their normal daily routines without any specific exercise program. The exercise group accomplished three 50-minute sessions, consisting of a 15-minute warm-up, 20-minute aerobics, and a 15-minute cool-down period. After twelve weeks, the exercise group improved significantly in cardiorespiratory endurance (half-mile walk test), in the sit-and-stand test (the number of times over thirty seconds a person could stand from a sitting position), and in agility, body fat, and balance. In addition, the nonexercisers were found to have a 4 percent loss on the half-mile walk time, a loss of 6 percent on tests of motor control and coordination, and a loss of 3 percent on agility.[12]

Since muscular weakness in the elderly contributes to an instability of gait that frequently leads to falling, more and more studies are pointing out the advantages of muscle-building exercises for the elderly. One group of investigators studied thirty-six elderly women (average age sixty-seven) who were already exercising aerobically three times a week. The group was divided in half—eighteen switched to resistance machines and eighteen continued to do aerobic exercise three times a week as before. After twenty-four weeks, the group using the resistance machines increased their weightlifting ability between 5 percent and 65 percent, improved their muscle mass, and reduced body fat; the control group exhibited none of these added benefits.[13]

Emotional and Mental Benefits of Regular Exercise

Evans and Rosenberg noted that those who continue to vigorously exercise in middle age have a better chance of living into their seventies, as they not only are more flexible and stronger but are also more self-reliant and self-confident.[14] Other investigators have substantiated these findings and have related exercise to increased imagination, intelligence, forthrightness, and concentration.[15]

There is some evidence that aged persons involved in regular physical activity show a surprising improvement in mental acuity. Such improvement could keep individuals out of nursing homes. In 1988, work by Theodore R. Bashore and colleagues suggests that fitness in the aging may slow the decline of the cognitive processes (such as the rate of mental processing) and in some cases improve them. He describes studies in which response speeds of older, aerobically fit subjects are higher than those of sedentary peers. In some cases the older, fit subjects' response speeds approach the speed of young adults.[16] According to the National Institute on Aging the estimated cost in the year 1992 for maintaining an individual in a long-term facility was $25,000 per year. At that rate the total cost for all patients in this category in the United States is $74 billion every year.

It must be recognized that a sizable number of people are handicapped and are thus limited in the type of aerobic exercise they can perform. Some have chronic and others have short-term disabilities. Physicians will, after a thorough medical evaluation, try to determine if the condition can be corrected medically. Is surgery needed to bring about the changes necessary to permit an effective training program? Can the patient walk at all? After an injury or arthritis flare-up it is medically imperative to restore a person's ability to walk as soon as possible. The inability to walk constitutes a medical "semi-emergency" as far as I'm concerned.

Jim, a fifty-year-old executive in a local computer store, sprained his ankle doing his walk/jog routine one evening. He arrived a few weeks later at the office walking with a cane. He asked, "Guess what happened?" I replied, "You were exercising at night as usual and did not see a pothole and sprained your ankle." "That's right," he said, "But guess what else happened?" My answer was, "You weren't able to work out because of your sprained ankle and you gained ten pounds in three weeks." "That's right," he said. "I've gained ten pounds, though my diet never changed."

Believe it or not exercise is strongly recommended even for organ transplant patients because it results in better conditioning after prolonged inactivity, increased confidence, and decreased incidence of osteoporosis and muscle atrophy caused by prednisone or other chemicals used to prevent organ rejection. The U.S. Transplant Games held at U.C.L.A. in 1992 offered an opportunity for such people to meet and compete. Competitions were held in swimming, track, tennis, and basketball, to name a few of the events. The winning time for the mile run was 4:58.

So much of the body temple's wholeness is related to exercise that all manner of energy must be directed to getting a person back to his or her aerobic program as soon as possible. A number of years ago, at the Eastern Intercollegiate Swimming Championships, I watched with awe and admiration as a swimmer stood on one leg (the other having been amputated) at the start of the 1,500-yard freestyle finals. He demonstrated that a handicapped person, with the help of extensive training, good coaching, and strong motivation, can overcome adversity.

Likewise, getting a patient back into the appropriate exercise program often requires a team effort. This team may comprise orthopedic surgeons, podiatrists, physical therapists, rheumatologists, dietitians, as well as the encouraging and enthusiastic family doctor. When directing people to begin a fitness program, especially older folks, it is helpful for the health-care providers to have firsthand knowledge of the community's fitness opportunities, such as the YMCA and senior fitness programs as well as U.S. Masters programs in swimming, running, skiing, rowing, biking, tennis, or squash.

Watching the transformation of an overweight, deconditioned, forty-five or fifty-year-old smoker into a vigorous, trim, non-smoking individual can be one of the most satisfying experiences in all of medicine. To see muscle replace fat, to see depression lift, to see people once cut off from their community enjoy improved and new relationships and a restoration of self-worth, to see them reach out to help others, and all of this culminating in a wholeness not present before—this is nothing short of a miracle! Such a transformation can be achieved in many cases with little or no prescription medicine.

Finding Time for Exercise

Harriet, a thirty-three-year-old mother of four children, has been struggling, for the past fifteen years that I've known her as a patient, with obesity and concomitant hypertension. She gained several pounds after delivering each of her children and was not able to lose that weight, which resulted in her being forty pounds over her former, ideal weight. She found it difficult to get time away from her young children long enough to jog or join an aerobic class with regularity. Part of a health-care provider's task is to try to fit an aerobic program into a busy person's life. She and I agreed upon a treadmill after thoroughly checking her current medical condition. The home treadmill allowed her to watch the children or be within earshot and still get a good workout. The machine's difficulty level was adjusted so that by the time she finished one half hour she felt "pleasantly out of breath." Within seven weeks, she had lost fifteen pounds and at the end of three months, she was down a total of thirty pounds. She became so energized and enthusiastic about her newly discovered body that she often added a two- to three-mile walk to her workout whenever the opportunity presented itself (usually two to three times a week). I can't remember her looking and feeling so well. She developed a better self-image and her blood pressure returned to normal as she lost weight. She now enjoys peace of mind, which can at least partially be attributed to the release of tension she experiences as she exercises. Her mind, body, and spirit (the body temple) all have been transformed.

The problem of finding time for exercise was successfully resolved in Harriet's case, but everyone's situation is different. We all have responsibilities that seem to leave very little space for this important activity. A few people get up early in the morning, walk their two miles before breakfast, and then go off to work. Those that have a more set work schedule and are allowed an hour or forty-five-minute lunch break, can skip the long lunch, eating a bagel or apple at their desk, change their work shoes for their jogging shoes, and jog away. Exercise dampens the appetite for many, so being hungry during the afternoon work time is often not a problem. Also, aerobic walking has an energizing effect, which can help us be more alert instead of experiencing the well-known post-lunch fatigue. Many people keep their jogging shoes in their cars. On the drive home they find a nice location to walk, blow off the day's tensions, and then drive home. Gyms and exercise clubs have the benefits of a large gathering of people, a variety of equipment, professional instruction, and a weatherproof location.

I've been collecting a long list of reasons "Why I didn't exercise today." Among them: the train or bus from work broke down; it's time to get or prepare dinner; or I'm just too tired. Others include the dog ate my jogging shoes; there are too many or not enough cars; I look bad in a jogging outfit; or it's too hot, cold, snowing, or raining. I'm always looking for more reasons to add to the list. I do not recommend aerobic exercise right before bed, as one will often be "blessed" with so much energy from the exercise that, while lying in bed looking at the ceiling at 3 o'clock in the morning, one has thoughts of getting up and washing the kitchen floor.

There has been a deluge of older athletes in the media of late. These athletes are accomplishing more than the public ever dreamed possible for people of their age. For example, at age forty-one, Jimmy Connors was drubbing players much younger than he as he advanced to the semifinals in the U.S. Open Tennis Championships in New York. He was finally beaten by a player almost twenty years younger in August 1991. The incredible pitching of forty-four-year-old Nolan Ryan of the Texas Rangers has also drawn great media attention. He pitched a no-hitter in May 1991 against Toronto, striking out sixteen players in a row. Toronto was then the best-hitting team in the major leagues.[17] Then there is Jim Law, who, at the age of sixty-five, broke the world record in track for seniors in the 400 meters and, at the same meet, became the new American senior record holder for 100- and 200-meter distances. His record in the 400 meters is 58.89 seconds; the world record is 43.29 seconds.[18] Other "older" athletes who have performed with outstanding ability lately are Mark Spitz (age forty-one), swimmer; George Foreman (age forty-two), boxer; and Sugar Ray Leonard (age thirty-four), boxer.

Bill Specht, class of 1980 at Princeton University, is a personal friend and was a nationally ranked swimmer in the butterfly stroke in college. For many years after graduation he held the Princeton pool record for that event. In the summer of 1993, at the U.S. Masters Swimming National Championships at Santa Clara, California, he entered six events and broke the world record for his age group in all six events. He was later featured in "Faces in the Crowd" in *Sports Illustrated* for this unusual accomplishment. Here are his times in college and at the meet thirteen years later:

	1980	1993
100-yard butterfly	48.8 seconds	50.3 seconds
200-yard butterfly	1:47.6	1:50.5
100-yard backstroke	52.7	51.9
200-yard backstroke	1:57.0	1:53.4

Bill is married and has a lovely wife and three children and trains in the early morning before work where he lives in Florida. His is another example of "holding back the ravages of old age."

Some studies show that nonexercising individuals have lost up to 40 percent of their strength and 10 percent of their muscle mass by the time they reach age sixty-five.[19] Arno Jensen from the Cooper Clinic in Dallas substantiates that poor nutrition and lack of exercise can be the cause of much of the physical disorders of aging. More and more research data is beginning to demonstrate the big gap between one's chronological age and one's physiological age.

Many studies have confirmed the importance of combining aerobic exercise with weight training at any age. As with all exercise programs, it is important to be checked over by one's physician before starting. When beginning weight training, get advice first. Start with lighter weights; you can use a machine or free weights (such as barbells or dumbbells). Gradually add resistance (or greater weight) until 3 sets of 10 to 15 repetitions fatigues the muscle. Rest for a minute between each set. As your strength increases add more weight so that you can do only sets of 6 to 10 repetitions. After several workouts at this level increase your number of reps to 10 to 15. Continue increasing weight and then repetitions gradually over time. At some point you will decide that further addition of weights is unnecessary. Then it's up to you to maintain your gains. You may want to switch around your routine, performing different exercises for the same muscle groups on different days, as muscles can "get used to" the same motion over and over. It is best to start each training period by warming up with lighter weights for a dozen easily performed reps and stretching before getting into the workout in earnest. This is where some advice and guidance is helpful.

William Evans states, "All the old fears about resistance training have turned out to be myths: lifting weights won't make you less flexible, cause or worsen hypertension, slow your speed, or wreck your back."[20] An ideal program includes three days a week of weight training and four days of aerobic training, with each session forty-five minutes to one hour in duration. Those competing in some of the Masters programs may have to alter the emphasis and the duration of the aerobic and weight training to fit their needs. Although no one is ready to concede that regular exercise lengthens the lifespan, most everyone does agree that quality of life can dramatically improve and the ability to avoid physical dependence upon others can be significantly reduced. I can recall a number of instances of having close games of squash with men thirty years younger than I and losing to men ten years older, demonstrating the advantage of keeping in shape with regular exercise throughout one's life. A 1991 chart in *Time* neatly shows that if we exercise regularly our stamina peaks around age twenty-eight or twenty-nine and can be preserved until about thirty-five. Then there is a 1 percent deterioration per year. Strength, on the other hand, reaches its pinnacle around the ages of thirty-eight to forty-two, with a subsequent loss per year of less than 1 percent. Lastly, good coordination can be preserved in the athlete well into his or her fifties with a subsequent loss of less than .4 percent per year.[21]

How is *your* body temple doing? Are you making the best use of all your gifts? These are questions for all of us to reflect upon from time to time. Having noted the many benefits of aerobic exercise, those giving all this advice (especially health-care providers) must also exhibit good health habits or risk losing credibility. This point is made by Paul:

> So I do not run aimlessly, nor do I box as though beating the air; but I punish my body and enslave it, so that after proclaiming to others I myself should not be disqualified.
> —1 Corinthians 9:26–27

I hope the reader now clearly understands the importance of regular exercise; it is the best health investment one can make in these days of high medical expenses. Everyone benefits—the individual, with an enhanced sense of well-being and the taxpayer, with lower medical costs.

10

The Handicapped Body Temple

T he U.S. Census Bureau reports that about 8 percent of Americans between the ages of sixteen and sixty-four have some form of handicap that interferes with their ability to move about in a normal manner. National Handicapped Sports, an organization devoted to athletic participation for handicapped people, listed eighty-six chapters in 1992, an increase from fifty-four in 1987. There are a growing number of sports for competing as well as recreational athletes who are handicapped. Part of this growth is the result of a general appreciation of the role of fitness in a healthy body temple and part is the result of improvements in prosthetic limbs. Wheelchairs used in sports such as racing, tennis, and basketball, for example, weigh as little as twelve pounds, being constructed of lightweight materials such as aluminum, titanium, and carbon fiber. More than 4,000 athletes competed in the ninth Paralympics in Barcelona in September 1992. At this writing, there are fifteen American organizations devoted to helping the handicapped engage in athletic activities.[1]

Whether competing in wheelchair basketball or painting a landscape using a brush clutched between the teeth, most of the handicapped I've met share at least one quality: an indomitable spirit.

The Strength of the Human Spirit:
A Patient Called Marion

It never ceases to amaze me the way the handicapped, including those with a terminal illness, cope in the midst of seemingly overwhelming odds. The human spirit can be a source of great strength for those afflicted and a wonderful inspiration for those in contact with these patients. Marion was a fifty-nine-year-old retired medical secretary. She had worked for many years cheerfully and efficiently in a busy dentist's office. A few years ago she developed a cancer of the intestines, which required surgery followed by radiation treatments and chemotherapy. Over the subsequent months many complications developed that left her with tubes in each kidney that drained into a bag, a gaping abdominal wound that was not healing well, and most of her insides gone. She was nourished through a stomach tube and intravenous feedings. She suffered frequent infections and multiple body chemistry imbalances. Despite this apparent collapse of the body temple, her face radiated with an overwhelming serenity. The entire staff taking care of her were struck how well she coped with the devastation of her physical body. From previous conversations with her over many years, I had realized she was a very spiritual person, and we had often talked about the healing power of prayer. Now here she was a patient herself in the intensive care unit of the hospital. During one of my visits to her bedside, I thanked her for giving us a wonderful gift. She thought a minute and then replied, "What is the gift you are speaking about?" When I answered, "Your gift of inner peace that you give to all of us taking care of you," she smiled and softly said, "Praise God." She died peacefully a few days later from an overwhelming blood stream infection. The spiritual part of Marion's body temple increasingly compensated for the deteriorating physical part and was a beacon of light despite the ongoing disintegration of her physical organs. The following quote from scripture reminded me of Marion's situation:

> For we know that if the earthly tent we live in is destroyed, we have a building from God, a house not

made with hands, eternal in the heavens. . . . For while we are still in this tent, we groan under our burden, because we wish not to be unclothed but to be further clothed, so that what is mortal may be swallowed up by life.

—2 Corinthians 5:1,4

And again, Paul writes:

Therefore I am content with weaknesses, insults, hardships, persecutions, and calamities for the sake of Christ; for whenever I am weak, then I am strong.

—2 Corinthians 12:10

The Marathon Runner with a Nailed Hip

Larry is a seventy-eight-year-old retired banker who started jogging about fifteen years ago. He had been on his college's track team, but then along came a busy professional life leaving him with "no time for exercise." During the subsequent thirty-five years while building a home, raising a family, and progressing in his career, Larry gained an enormous amount of weight—70 pounds to be exact, a far cry from the weight of the thin runner of college days. As his girth increased, his joints began hurting. He was out of breath with the slightest bit of exertion. With medical clearance, he started a slow jogging program and joined a local running club. He greatly enjoyed being with a varied age group, and he was one of the senior members. By paying attention to diet and by being disciplined enough to exercise regularly, he steadily lost weight. In a few years, his weight fell from 210 to 138 pounds, the latter being similar to his college weight.

Over the past several years, he has run in twenty-six marathons. One of the more recent was the Berlin Marathon, in which he ran past the downed Berlin Wall (the race traversed both the east and west sides soon after the wall was demolished). He ran this race after undergoing surgery for a fractured hip, which had occurred after tripping on a sidewalk. In addition to the Berlin Marathon, he finished four marathons in the U.S. I dare say there are not too many men running marathons with nailed hips at the age of seventy-eight! Larry's life seems to have been transformed by his lifestyle of daily exercise. He does not take any medicines; he has regained his vitality and self-esteem and reflects a very positive outlook on life. Larry illustrates the ability to overcome the potential handicaps of age and hip surgery and to go beyond them and successfully live life in a positive manner.

Courage, Brain Cancer, and the New York City Marathon

Fred Lebow and Grete Waitz finished the 1992 New York City Marathon together, taking five-and-one-half hours to complete the course. What is so astounding about this? you may ask. Fred was the "guru" of runners in the New York area. His presence had been felt for many years, and he had been one of the leading proponents for running as a way of life. The 1992 race was a celebration of life—his life—as he had recently finished two years of chemotherapy for brain cancer. In addition, Fred was celebrating his sixtieth birthday. Equally touching was the fact that his running partner, Grete Waitz, (who is about thirty years younger), was a nine-times winner of the very same New York Marathon. A moving photograph in the *New York Times* showed them finishing the race together accompanied by several friends. The photo captured Fred's unbeatable spirit and served as an inspiration for others. Grete, on the other hand, put her own competitive emotions aside allowing her to give a heartfelt salute to her longtime friend. It is a touching story about two special people.

Handicapped Skiers

While skiing in Colorado recently, I was pleasantly surprised to see a ski school for the physically handicapped. The handicapped skiers went down the slopes a number of ways depending upon the nature of the handicap. Each skier was accompanied by an instructor. When both lower extremities were not functioning or absent, the individual sat on a narrow sled using his or her arms. Each hand held small skis as aids in maintaining balance. The joy and wonder of it all struck many of us as we watched the handicapped fly down the slopes. They seemed happy and confident; the beautiful Colorado sky and clear air were very much a part of their day, as they were for the rest of us. At the bottom of the slope the attendants were well trained in the technique of lifting the sled and its occupant onto the chairlift as well as helping remove the sled at the top. The philosophy of the Crested Butte Physically Challenged Ski Program (CBPCSP) is to encourage the development of skills for skiing and the traits of self-awareness, confidence, and trust—which are all useful building blocks for coping with life's challenges. This nonprofit program has been in operation since 1987 and is supported by many in the community. During that same visit I saw skiers with other handicaps, including the visually impaired, who were guided downhill by instructors. Everyone seemed to greatly enjoy the experience. The body temple components (mind, body, and spirit) were all interacting as a unit. It seemed as though the physical imperfections were compensated for by the sheer joy of being part of that beautiful day's activities. This experience helped to create a wholeness that these men and women might not have realized in a less stimulating environment. The ski program must be a great source of encouragement and fond memories for those who participate.

Works of Art amidst Multiple Handicaps

Celia had been a gifted painter and sculptor all her life, and by the age of eighty she had exhibited her works throughout the United States and in Europe. Toward the end of her life, her hands were so badly deformed by arthritis that she could barely wield the mallet. Her hearing was very severely impaired and only through lip reading and double hearing aids could she hear. Her sight was equally bad—so bad that she required a large magnifying glass fitted to a stand on a table as an aid to her thick glasses in order to see her work. Despite these handicaps, she joyfully conducted classes and published a book illustrating much of her work. She continued to work until one week before she died suddenly from a stroke. Again, although the aging process chipped away at her physical self, this was compensated for by her personal charisma and contagious enthusiasm.

In many cases we cannot overcome adversity without God's grace—a gift from God to us. Sadly, we are often too busy with our individual lives to sit quietly long enough to listen and meditate on what he is trying to tell us. By being quiet we will hear "that still, inner voice" and be led to do his will for us with thankful hearts and to appreciate his presence even in the busy times and places of our lives.

A Missed Opportunity for Knee Surgery

Not everyone takes advantage of modern medicine's advances. A mechanic friend of mine, Jerry, who is seventy-seven-years-old, is such an example. Though a strong man, he has in the past few years become progressively more crippled with severe arthritis of both knees. This has reached the point where he needs two crutches to get around and has been forced to sell his gas station. Despite endless discussions with me and others, he has steadfastly refused to consider surgery to implant artificial knee replacements. The continuous strain on his upper body of using crutches has resulted in his arms and back becoming more arthritic. It breaks my heart to see this man slowly being bent in two by this condition. However, he feels that arthritis runs in his family and that it is part of growing old. The physical part of Jerry's body temple is deteriorating, but, for one reason or another, his emotional and spiritual components do not appear to be compensating. I feel Jerry is both fearful of surgery and somewhat fatalistic about life, although his brother had a hip replacement and is doing fine.

Some folks are blessed by growing spiritually and emotionally through the pain when a physical component of the body temple breaks down. This growth is a gift of the Holy Spirit. An inner peace resides despite the handicap. Others who suffer a disability become depressed and decline spiritually and emotionally. The reasons for this are best known by God alone. I do not pretend to have all the answers.

Alcoholism Turned around by God's Grace

Alan developed a drinking problem in high school that became worse in college. He was forced to leave the university because of poor grades, yet he continued to suffer alcohol addiction. He subsequently hit bottom; he experienced memory blackouts, stopped eating, couldn't find work, and would have starved were it not for a local soup kitchen. Then one morning, while suffering a spell of memory loss at the ripe old age of twenty-two, he became so frightened that he joined AA. Over a period of many months while attending AA meetings four to five times a week, he reached the point of being able to return to church. He was experiencing God's grace at work. The Lord has since become the most important person in his life. Alan teaches Sunday school at a local church; he is no longer depressed; his sense of self-worth has returned; and he radiates a joy never present before. He has no difficulty in giving God all the credit for turning his life around. Alan has been sober for the past three years. He is very willing to talk to his friends about God's love as the force that turned him away from his self-destructive path. Such a statement is very powerful when it comes from a peer. This young man is now happily a whole person again in mind, body, and spirit and is at ease ordering a soft drink when out with his friends. I think we all have an "Alan" in our lives.

> O Lord my God, I cried to you for help,
> and you have healed me.
>
> O Lord, you brought up my soul from Sheol,
> restored me to life from among those gone
> down to the Pit.
> Sing praises to the Lord, O you his faithful ones, and
> give thanks to his holy name.
> —Psalm 30:2–4

A Substance Abuser Recovered

Ellen was also forced to leave college because of substance abuse. She entered another college the following year after she realized that she had to change her lifestyle or perish. Not only did she graduate with honors and give talks on drug abuse to local schoolchildren, but she currently is doing very well in her second year at a seminary studying for the clergy. She has restored her body temple to something more complete and radiant than it had ever been before.

So often family and friends feel helpless when they see a loved one abuse alcohol or drugs. Sometimes they can only be present, though feeling desperately frustrated and trying to intervene and guide the disturbed individual. These loved ones continue to pray despite the lack of any overt sign of progress. Then, one day, through God's grace, the individual becomes receptive to help, and things begin to turn around.

But truly it is the spirit in a mortal,
the breath of the Almighty, that makes for understanding."
                                                   –Job 32:8

Laurence Freeman, O.S.B., nicely relates the story of the Prodigal Son to the modern problem of drug abuse:

The parent's joy at the child's rehabilitation from drugs or alcohol more closely mirrors God than the moralist's condemnation or the church's penance. The "new life" of the gospel is the liberation from ignorance and the knowledge of the universal agape.[2]

A Grouchy Patient "Loved to Death"

Mary Agnes, an elderly woman in her late seventies, was plagued with a poor disposition; in fact, she was downright nasty. She exhibited this behavior at virtually every office encounter, always finding something to criticize. You might say she was a crank of the first order! With the full cooperation of the office staff, we decided that the only way for all of us to survive was to try to "love her to death." Hence, upon every encounter, we all would make a point to remark how nice she looked, how pretty her blouse was, especially with the matching necklace and the unusual pin that she wore, how energetic she appeared, how her broad-brim straw hat added such flair, and so forth. Before long, she started to open up and become chatty. She stopped complaining, even smiled at times, and, after more time had passed, she started to show us the warm and friendly side of her personality. A miracle seemed to be happening. We actually started to enjoy her visits, and we got the distinct impression that she was beginning to look forward to seeing us as well. She had changed!

As time passed, Mary Agnes became terminally ill, which resulted in her becoming housebound. She could no longer drive a car, she lived alone, and she found it difficult to find people to drive her to the office. It was at this point that I started to make regular house visits. (Many doctors make house calls on patients who are housebound, believe it or not.) Her medical problems started to take their toll, and progressively she became weaker and weaker. Despite her condition, she seemed to look forward to our visit, which had become a social encounter as much as anything else. Some cheese and a small glass of brandy were always neatly placed on a side table in her living room by her chair. Sensing her days were coming to a close, I began to visit her every few days on my way home. She would tell me about the things she had done as a young woman and the story of her family, and I would quietly listen. I always made sure to take her blood pressure and listen to her lungs and heart though I knew nothing more could really be done. "Being present" seemed all that was called for. More than once I thought, "Isn't this what life is all about?" She eventually died peacefully at home. I often reflect on this relationship as an example of "Who transformed whom?" Did she transform our attitude toward her, or did we transform her by deliberatively going out of our way to love her? Probably the truth lies somewhere in between. What a revelation it was for all of us! We all have a spiritual inner self that is a wonderful gift. But how many times do we allow ourselves to go beneath that crusty exterior to discover the real person often crying out to be loved? I believe the following speaks to the above true story.

A new heart I will give you, and a new spirit I will put within you; and I will remove from your body the heart of stone and give you a heart of flesh.

–Ezekiel 36:26

A Journey to Wholeness

Bill Irwin and his seeing-eye dog Orient, live in North Carolina. Bill is a lecturer, author, and publishes a newsletter, "The Orient Express." In 1968, at age twenty-eight, he lost vision in his left eye as the result of malignant melanoma, and it was removed. (His condition was later diagnosed as chorioretinitis.) In a few years the condition spread to his right eye and resulted in total blindness by 1976. In addition to this problem, Bill was trying to deal with alcoholism; he was divorced; and his three children had distanced themselves from him. Bill was despondent; he felt isolated and alone. In his book *Blind Courage,* Bill depicts his trek into the wilderness along the entire length of the Appalachian Trail with the help of his friend, Orient. He was the first person to accomplish this feat. Bill's was a journey to wholeness. His personal saga began in March 1990 at Springer Mountain, Georgia, and ended eight months and 2,167 miles later at Abol Bridge, Maine. Bill's perseverance, courage, and constant appreciation of God's presence and grace are inspiring. His experience involved all aspects of the body temple.

Whether we are literally in the wilderness or in a quiet place in our home, we all need daily time to be quiet and listen to what God is trying to tell us. As Bill remarks, "As the hike progressed, I sensed another dimension of the wilderness—the ability to spend time alone with God. Away from the noise and distractions of my normal life, I had a unique opportunity to listen. I hadn't requested this experience, so He must have known that I needed it."[3]

Down but Not Out

Joe is one of my favorite patients. He retired a few years ago after working for thirty years as an accountant for the state of

New Jersey. What makes him unusual is the fact that this seventy-four-year-old man contracted polio as a teenager and requires two crutches and leg braces to get around. During his working years, in order to get to his office, he would first grab the railing of the steps leading to the main entrance of the building. While working his way up the steps from the sidewalk, he would use this opportunity to greet his co-workers with a cheery "hello" or other upbeat comment. With every visit to our medical office, he would kid the nurses, tell a few corny jokes, but never once did he complain about his handicap. He, like so many individuals with handicaps, had long since learned techniques to master his environment, such as a specific way of getting up on the examining table, dressing without help, and generally moving about on his own. The only request he made of us was to hand him his crutches, and he then would place them within reach for when he needed them. The procedure was always the same: hang on to a solid object or crutches with one arm, shake out one leg so that the metal brace snapped with a bang into the locked position, and then follow the same procedure for the other leg. People watching him go through this well-rehearsed system and were actually more of a hazard to him if they tried to help him. He recalled one incident that illustrated this. He had just finished his dinner at a local restaurant and was starting his routine to get up from the table, when several ladies from a nearby table, over his protestations, started to lift him up by the arms. The more they lifted him, the more his legs (which were not locked in place) began to slide. The result was quite predictable as he gently eased down to the floor. "Then the fun really started to happen," he recalled, with a twinkle in his eye. "It was the first time I've ever had four nice women hanging over my neck at the same time. The manager and a busboy came to the rescue. I appreciated the humor, and I didn't hurt myself at all. It was quite a memorable evening!"

What a gift to be able to live, work, and enjoy life and to do so wholeheartedly!

From Bedbound to Walking: Persistence and Prayer

Jane Ann, a seventy-five-year-old strong and very independent widow, was in the hospital for several months suffering from low back pain. She had undergone two operations over the previous three years for severe back spasms caused by vertebral discs pinching the nerves in the lower back. For many weeks she could not sit or lie down or even stand for any length of time without suffering severe pain, which meant that she could not obtain proper rest. She was both exhausted and depressed. Every time I visited her she was reading the Bible—her only consolation. After many X-rays, the surgeon determined that the discs seemed not to be the trouble but that adhesions from prior surgeries were actually causing the pain. The day before the final surgery we prayed together that God would finally heal her. The days following surgery she happily noted the gradual disappearance of the pain in her back and legs. Although she was able to lie down and enjoy freedom from pain, she was not yet able to walk without considerable distress. She still required several weeks of therapy. Finally, after successfully completing the weeks of seemingly endless physiotherapy, she was well enough to come to the office for a follow-up visit. I watched her walk down the hall in the office, her face grinning from ear to ear, topped off by a snappy Tam O'Shanter hat, and carrying a cane over her shoulder much like a rifle.

In addition, Jane Ann had purposefully walked ten blocks from her home to my office as a way to say, "Thank you God for answered prayer!" This long-suffering patient experienced a miraculous transformation. We both said a prayer of gratitude, and, at the end of our visit, I requested that she walk next door to the hospital and go to the floor where she had for so long been ensconced. I knew the nurses who had helped her all those days would be thrilled to see her walk briskly down the hall (and I was certain they would love her hat). They were elated and could hardly believe their eyes! So many times health-care providers (especially nurses), don't get to appreciate the "finished product" of their hours of caring. I've always felt it is important for them to share in the celebration of healing, to rejoice in seeing the patient well once again. In sharing their healing, the newly well patient has the opportunity to thank all who helped in the healing process, and the nurses receive the often-needed assurance that their day-to-day work pays off.

We Christians, likewise, must share everyday victories to keep our faith strong and well. It is important in building our faith to know when God answers our prayers—it enables all of us to rejoice for this blessing. At times we also must continue to pray even when answers seem to be slow in coming. The Lord listened to Jane Ann's prayers. She never lost heart during those long, sleepless nights; she knew that God still had a perfect plan for her life. This faith is beautifully stated in Jeremiah.

> For surely I know the plans I have for you, says the Lord, plans for your welfare and not for harm, to give you a future with hope. Then when you call upon me and come and pray to me, I will hear you. When you search for me, you will find me; if you seek me with all your heart, I will let you find me, says the Lord.
>
> –Jeremiah 29:11–14

11

Aging and Osteoporosis

I t has been estimated that 25 million people are afflicted with osteoporosis in the U.S. The majority are women. The disease is characterized by an excessive loss of calcium from the bones culminating in holes or porous openings. This is what the term *osteoporosis* means (*osteo,* "bone" and *poros,* "pore"). Interest in this condition has risen in recent years because people are living longer and are thus more likely to get the disease. Dr. Robert Marcus of Stanford University reports that osteoporosis is usually diagnosed following a fracture (often caused by a fall) and is noted as an incidental finding after performing the X-ray. In women, these fractures increase in frequency five to fifteen years after menopause.[1] A history of osteoporosis in one's mother and grandmother may increase the likelihood of suffering this disease, as it may be genetically inherited.

Bone density is the primary factor determining whether a given bone will fracture during a fall. There are three common fracture sites: vertebrae (44 percent), hip (19 percent), and wrist (14 percent). The latter is called a Colles fracture and involves the lower end of the radius bone. As there are approximately 1.1 million fractures caused by falls every year in the U.S., this breaks down to 500,000 fractures of the vertebrae, 250,000 hip fractures, and 200,000 wrist fractures.[2] Treating these injuries costs $1 billion yearly, and if the cost of medical care is added to the lost income, the total estimated cost is about $6 billion annually.[3] As one third of women and one sixth of men over sixty-five years of age are likely to be victims of hip fracture, the enormity of the problem is clear.

Bone Remodeling

The term *bone remodeling* refers to the process whereby bone is constantly reabsorbed (broken down) and reformed (renewed) by the body. Cells that cause bone reabsorption are called osteoclasts, and those that reform bone are called osteoblasts. After age thirty-five, in both men and women, bone loss becomes more predominant than bone formation. The normal internal honeycomb-like structure of the bone dilates with the aging process, which produces larger holes. Over time the bones lose mass and strength. As the bones become more porous and lose calcium, they become more prone to fractures. The loss of estrogen in menopausal women exaggerates the loss of calcium further. Weight-bearing exercise (such as walking or running) appears to benefit bone health. Those who have been in a cast that greatly hinders walking, for example, develop rapid loss of bone density, whereas those who devote a lifetime to an aerobic program that involves weight-bearing activity maintain a higher bone density. There is some evidence that swimming (which is not weight-bearing), by pulling on tendons and muscle groups that stress the bones, also benefits bone health. Some researchers have reported that the combination of weight training and aerobic exercise resulted in greater bone density than aerobic training alone.[4] Dr. Mehrsheed Sinaki from the Mayo Clinic feels that it is possible that a high level of physical activity started when young and continued throughout life may build up and preserve a "bank of skeletal mass" that would be available in later life when osteoporosis can become a problem.[5] It may therefore be best for girls to start taking calcium and to be active in weight-bearing activities to build up bone density at a young age.

The average American woman consumes about 450–550 mg. of calcium daily; the recommended daily allowance for a premenopausal woman is 1,000 mg. per day and for a postmenopausal woman is 1,500 mg. per day. Three glasses of milk provides about 900 mg. of calcium, but, because of the frequent occurrence of lactose intolerance in older people, calcium tablets can be used to avert this problem. Exercise, both impact (walking and jogging) and nonimpact (weightlifting and swimming), will help to build bone calcium. A point to remember is that women who exercise or train heavily (such as marathon runners) may exercise to the point of amenorrhea (suppression of menstruation) by reducing body fat too much, and may actually lose the benefits of estrogen. Their bones would thus not resemble those of a contemporary but the bones of a woman in her fifties.

Patients with organ transplants may also be vulnerable to osteoporosis because they often require the taking of steroids as well as chemotherapy to prevent rejection of the transplanted organ. Both of these medications can contribute to bone density loss.

In one study, male weightlifters and a group of male and female ballet dancers had greater bone density than their healthy counterparts in the control group. Even though the type of exercise differed, the regularity of the exercise benefited bone health. Recent research reports that combining exercise with calcium supplements may lessen bone loss exercise plus estrogen treatment may actually increase bone density.[6]

Dr. Marcus advocates estrogen replacement for post-menopausal patients both to prevent bone loss and to take advantage of the heart-protecting effect. The latter benefit is thought to be due to the rise in blood HDL (high density lipoprotein, the "good" cholesterol), which cleans up cholesterol in the blood. However, there are contraindications to estrogen treatment such as a history of breast cancer, active endometriosis, or development of a lung clot (embolus) while taking oral contraceptives. It is always wise to consult one's physician thoroughly before undertaking such a regimen, as every woman is unique. She must feel physically as well as emotionally at ease with the treatment. Although the addition of a progesterone agent reduces the risk of cancer of the uterus and may reduce bone loss, such treatment may decrease the benefit to the heart. Marcus goes on to say that calcium alone may be best if a woman has any of the contraindications to hormone therapy.[7]

There is still controversy in this field. Some investigators feel the "best of all worlds" for menopausal women consists in the combination of exercise, adequate calcium intake, and estrogen repletion. Under such conditions, exercise is responsible for stimulating the bone remodeling process, calcium supplements are incorporated into the new bone, and estrogen prevents excessive loss of bone. They cite that it is otherwise too difficult to keep up with the 2 to 4 percent bone loss that can occur every year after menopause.[8] Another approach being considered is the consumption of a calcitonin (a nonestrogen that retards bone loss) supplement. Calcitonin, like estrogen, reduces bone reabsorption and also seems to reduce the pain of collapsed vertebrae. Fluoride supplements have been examined as a possible treatment, but this probably has too many side-effects. Vitamin D complements calcium in helping to prevent osteoporosis; 800 to 1,000 units per day should be sufficient, as doses higher than this may promote the formation of kidney stones. Obese women may experience fewer cases of osteoporosis both because they bear more weight and because fat may attract estrogen and increase the body's store of it. On the other hand, obese people, being more subject to arthritis of the weight-bearing joints, are less likely to exercise. There appears to be a higher incidence of osteoporosis among whites and Asians than blacks. Slower bone turnover in blacks may account for this. It is generally agreed that smoking cancels the benefits of estrogen replacement. Other factors that can hasten the development of osteoporosis by inhibiting calcium absorption are alcohol abuse, excessive caffeine consumption, heparin, antacids with aluminum, excess thyroid activity, and cortisone and its derivatives.

Bent Body; Unbroken Spirit

Alice has been a bit bent over all the twenty years I've known her as a patient. She is now close to eighty years old, and her posture seems to worsen with each passing year. Her torso is now almost parallel to the ground when she walks. However, her inner glow and joy for life are so much a part of her existence that at each encounter my attention is immediately directed to her happy spirit rather than her twisted body. She has suffered from a series of collapsed vertebrae (compression fractures), caused by a lack of sufficient calcium in her bones. Although the increased interest in osteoporosis, a disease from which she suffers, may find treatments for this affliction, I doubt if anything can be done for her at this late date. It is probably too late for her to build up bone mass and much too late to straighten out her fractured and distorted vertebrae. Besides, she does not suffer any pain and has a host of grandchildren who worship her "just as she is."

Isn't it wonderful to love someone for their inner beauty, which so often outshines any physical impairment? The radiating joy that comes forth from the distorted body is really a gift, a gift from God. Alice reminds us that truly "beauty is in the eyes of the beholder"—her inner beauty shines so strongly that it overwhelms her distorted body. The very act of struggling with a handicap so often brings out a hidden depth of strength and tenderness that under other circumstances might lie dormant and hidden from the rest of the world. Much the same could be said about a personal crisis, a time of brokenness, when one dies to one's self and learns to trust in the Lord's plan rather than one's own. Such times bring out a different person, one who grows in God's grace and learns that inner peace comes from experiencing God's love personally. One then can glorify him by reaching out to others. Like all of us, Alice has three parts to her body temple. The physical component may be distorted, but her emotional and spiritual parts more than make up for her disability. She never complains about the effects of her osteoporosis but instead goes on and leads as full a life as anyone her age. Would modern treatments started as a young girl have made a difference in her condition? I would hope so. Would she be such a powerful source of love and radiant joy to others without this handicap? I wonder.

12

Nutrition and the Body Temple

There has been too much fat in the average American diet for many years, although overall nutrition is improving. Many of us raised in the 1940s and 1950s remember having eggs almost every day, butter, ice cream frequently, cheese, whipped cream, hot dogs, and hamburgers all as regular fare day in and day out. Fast foods, more common today than previously, account for 38 percent of the fat content in the American diet. Excess fat appears to be related to excess risk of cancer of the breast, colon, and prostate as well as cardiovascular disease. A fatty acid essential for growth is linoleic acid (an unsaturated fat found in many oils, such as peanut oil). It is now accepted, however, that linoleic acid enhances cancer of the breast, pancreas, and colon in rodents.[1] Human nutrition is a complex issue; thus physicians have found it quite difficult to make strong recommendations for avoiding certain foods. Oftentimes a substance, when tested on animals, can both induce disease and, under other conditions, protect from disease.

What we know is this: our diet should be low fat (less than 30 percent of total daily calories) and high in complex carbohydrates such as potatoes and pasta (70 percent of total daily calories). Cholesterol consumption should be less than 200 mg. per day. We should decrease saturated fat, which is found in chocolate, butter, egg yolks, coconut oils, bacon, and palm oils and replace them with polyunsaturated fat, which is found in sunflower and olive oils and margarine made from liquid oils. Increasing the amount of fiber in our diet not only helps prevent constipation but also can help prevent cancer of the colon as well as reduce serum cholesterol levels. Fiber gives bulk to the stool allowing a better cleansing of the colon. It thereby prevents cancer-producing material in the stool from remaining in contact with the wall of the colon for long periods of time. The nitrates found in food prepared by charcoal grilling, if consumed daily, may be responsible for some cancers of the colon. Examples of foods especially high in fiber are whole grain cereals and breads, pinto and kidney beans, raspberries, and peas.

Excessive cholesterol in our diet can damage our coronary arteries. Circulating low-density lipoproteins (LDL, the "bad" cholesterol) are oxidized by substances in the bloodstream and appear inside of cells within the walls of coronary arteries. These cells consider the oxidized LDL a foreign substance, something not normally found in the circulation, and so surround and isolate this troublesome molecule, much in the way a wooden splinter is walled off under the skin. The oxidized LDL cells inside the coronary artery wall stimulate the migration of monocytes to the area of inflammation. These monocytes are capable of being transformed into macrophages, cells that act as scavengers. Macrophages secrete substances that stimulate the growth of smooth muscle cells and help break down local tissue. The end result is the incorporation of cellular debris, cholesterol particles, and other fatty breakdown products within each macrophage, which is then called a "foam cell." This is thought to be the precursor of the arteriosclerotic plaque. The consensus of ongoing research is that arteriosclerosis is some sort of inflammatory process. The plaque over time enlarges and eventually encroaches upon the lumen of the coronary artery. The repeated inflammatory process of injury and healing leads to the narrowing of the coronary lumens and to plaque formation, which culminates in coronary artery disease. This process is greatly enhanced when the patient has increased amounts of cholesterol in the blood. Vitamins E, C, and betacarotenoids are "antioxidants" and appear to prevent this reaction or greatly ameliorate it. There is, therefore, keen interest in the role of antioxidants not only as powerful tools in the prevention of heart disease but also in the treatment of certain types of cancer.

Interest has also been shown in the role vitamins play in chronic disease prevention. "I believe the evidence is very good that vitamins C, E, and betacarotene play important roles in preventing chronic diseases like cancer and heart disease," said Dr. Gladys Block, professor of epidemiology and public health nutrition at the University of California, Berkeley.[2] Vitamin A encourages normal cell growth and seems to play an important role in the process described above, even though it is not an antioxidant. Some recent research suggests that vitamins E and C and selenium might be beneficial in warding off colon cancer and that vitamin A may help prevent colon and breast cancer.[3]

I have been excited at the prospect of a vitamin-zinc combination that may help delay the formation of and in some cases eliminate cataracts. At this writing, six patients of mine were told to return in two years for cataract surgery, and at the appointed time of return the cataracts were gone.

It is felt that "free radicals" or molecules that shoot out in all directions from our body cells are looking for a missing electron to "calm them down." These molecules oxidize cells as they hit our various organs causing the cells to grow atypically. When the molecules strike the lens of the eye, the lens can be oxidized, which can create cataracts. Antioxidants, it is thought, supply the sought-after electrons that the free radicals need, which then leads to this "calming down" effect. There is mounting evidence that antioxidants play a role in helping the body's defenses against tumor growth, cataract formation, and coronary artery disease. I realize the story of the six cataract patients is anecdotal. Medical literature, nevertheless, is beginning to note the possible benefits of this treatment. Time will tell. There still is much about vitamins that we don't fully understand.

Calcium Consumption in the Elderly

Few elderly Americans consume enough calcium. Calcium absorption becomes less efficient as we age; significantly inefficient in women in their sixties and men in their seventies. Milk products are the best way to attain the estimated 1,500 mg. daily requirement for older people. Foods high in calcium are cheese, yogurt, salmon, kale, and turnips. Although some people may need calcium tablets, the calcium citrate form seems to be preferable over the calcium carbonate form. Calcium carbonate may cause constipation, abdominal bloating, and hyperactivity. Calcium citrate is better absorbed, especially in the elderly, whose stomachs often lack sufficient acid. It also has fewer gastrointestinal side effects.

Nourishing the Weak and Frail

I often see patients who are frail, malnourished, and weak, with failing appetites. This condition leads to vitamin, protein, and mineral deficiencies as well as dehydration, poor kidney function, and medication build-up in the body, which can further lead to drug toxicity. Unfortunately, the scenario often worsens as a vicious circle of weakness and decreased intake of nourishment leads to more drug side effects and subsequent weight loss and weakness. Intravenous fluids are usually required to correct dehydration. Occasionally nasal-gastric tubes are employed short-term to improve the nutritional status of patients. When nutritional needs are severe or when the patient cannot swallow food (following a stroke, for example) a "peg" is used that connects a small tube from the outside of the abdomen directly to the stomach. Highly nutritious solutions can thereby be delivered and absorbed directly into the stomach. Pegs can be used for many months if necessary.

The Dietary Needs of Athletes

Physicians interested in sports medicine recommend at least two quarts of fluids a day. It is best not to count caffeine drinks as part of this amount since caffeine can act as a diuretic and actually cause a net loss of fluid. At least two to three hours before an athletic event, one should eat a meal that is low in fat, high in carbohydrates, and moderate in protein. Fat, which is absorbed slowly, should be avoided. Even protein takes two to three hours to be absorbed. Bread, on the other hand, is usually absorbed in one hour or less, and so complex carbohydrates such as bread and pasta may be the best choice near the time of the event.

Physicians specializing in sports medicine recommend that athletes eat three meals per day. If the time between meals is too long, blood sugar levels may drop, resulting in symptoms characteristic of hypoglycemia: sudden dizziness, weakness, sweating, and great hunger. These symptoms may contribute to poor athletic performance. There are a number of "high performance" drinks that are purported to increase athletic performance by replenishing an athlete's depleted fluids, electrolytes (sodium, potassium, and chloride), and calories. The most important thing to remember is to replenish the fluid volume during training and during long-distance running or prolonged aerobic performances. Researchers in this field stress the necessity of adequate calorie intake.

Counting Fat Calories

In *The Choose to Lose Diet,* authors Dr. Ron Goor, Nancy Goor, and Katherine Boyd make this comment, "The word is FAT. FAT is what you don't want to be and FAT is what you ate to become FAT. So, the way to become NOT FAT is to reduce fat in your diet. Don't focus on total calories . . . or sugar . . . or starch. Focus on FAT."[4] One of my favorite tricks when talking about diets with patients is to hold two teaspoons, one in each hand. I ask the individual to imagine that one teaspoon contains grandmother's favorite juicy homemade strawberry jam and the other "ultra-light, no cholesterol" margarine. Then I ask, "Which of the two teaspoons has more calories?" Almost without fail, the male patients and a fair number of the female patients will choose the teaspoon containing the thick jam. This, of course, is wrong because margarine contains 9 calories per gram of fat and jam contains only 4 calories per gram of sugar. Tricky, isn't it? So I'm learning to eat plain bread, no butter or margarine, and avoid my favorite peanut butter snacks, nuts, and other items such as potato chips as a regular treat (most of the time anyway). Goor, Goor, and Boyd go on to say, "It's your fat tooth, not your sweet tooth, that gets you into trouble."

As a general rule I've found over the years that among those who have lost weight, the ones who maintain the weight loss two years later are those who were exercising during the weight-losing process and, more important, continue to exercise after reaching their desired weight. Very frequently, those who stop their aerobic regimen upon reaching their weight reduction goal and discontinue the exercise regain their weight and may even exceed their starting weight. Needless to say, medical clearance is mandatory and guidance and encouragement are required before one starts the exercise part of the weight-loss program. The patient should see his or her physician every few months during the program. The physician will, among other things, exhort, encourage, guide, and praise the patient and may even intimidate in a constructive fashion. During every visit, I measure blood pressure, listen to heart and lungs, remind the patient to be "pleasantly out of breath" when finishing the half hour of aerobic exercise, and I personally weigh each patient. This practice has brought some humor especially when a man takes off his wristwatch before being weighed or a woman wears a light summer dress during a snowstorm because she knows that she, too, will have to step on "the meanest scales in town."

An interest in good nutrition as well as anxiety about pesticides have contributed to an increased awareness of what kinds of food we consume. The saying, "You are what you eat," has been proven true over and over. One wise man, especially revered by physicians, made this same point many centuries ago.

> Let food be your medicine and medicine be your food.
> Nature heals; the physician is only nature's assistant.
>
> –Hippocrates

Further Reading

Ron Goor, Nancy Goor, and Katherine Boyd, *The Choose to Lose Diet* (Boston: Houghton Mifflin Company, 1990).

I've been impressed by how often my patients feel it is necessary to watch the calories in sweets in order to lose weight. *The Choose to Lose Diet* correctly emphasizes the much higher calorie count in foods high in fat content. Though I feel exercise and diet are important factors in keeping weight under control, the former is probably more crucial than the latter. At the same time, the admonition, "You are FAT because you eat too much FAT," is worth remembering.

13

Psychological Aspects of Aging

Alzheimer's Disease and Forgetfulness

I t has been only in the past decade, as the population has aged and people have begun to live longer, that the country has truly become aware of the tragedy called Alzheimer's disease. It used to be called senility or hardening of the arteries, and today affects one out of twelve Americans over sixty-five and one in three over eighty years of age. SDAT (Senile dementia of the Alzheimer type), affects 60 percent of patients in chronic care facilities, and about 20 percent of Parkinson's disease patients develop this condition. Mini-strokes resulting in multi-infarct dementia may coexist in 15 percent of SDAT patients. The cost of treating SDAT is very great—about $40 billion for 1993. More women seem to be affected, probably because they live longer than men. One form of the disease manifests itself before age fifty-five and another form after age sixty-five. The former probably is genetically inherited and constitutes about one half of the cases. The latter type has no familial or genetic basis.[1] Recent studies reveal that amyloid (a protein-like material) accumulation is at the root of the problem. The accumulation is caused by a mutant amyloid precursor gene located on chromosome 21 in the familial form of SDAT. The gene causes the precursor to divide so that the amyloid is not metabolized (not used) but accumulates. Although this process applies only to the familial type of SDAT, it is being studied intensively.

The disease is progressive in its course. This degenerative process results in a considerable loss of brain cells from the brain cortex, hippocampus, and subcortical (midbrain) structures. Brain cells are replaced by senile plaques, consisting of dead and dying cells that surround a central core of amyloid, and by neurofibrillary tangles—spiral filaments found within brain cells (neurons). Although plaques and tangles are found in the normal aging process, in SDAT they are greatly increased. Acetylcholine needed for proper nerve transmission in the brain is diminished as well.[2] The damaged neurons produce far less acetylcholine and other enzymes used in transmitting neural impulses, which leads to failure of neurotransmitters and the resultant impairment of cognitive functions.

Viruses and other infectious agents as well as aluminum found in certain antacids have been investigated, but as yet no definite connection to SDAT has been firmly established.

The part of the brain concerned with short-term memory and emotions, known as the hippocampus, is affected quite early in the disease. It is not unusual for the patient to remember his or her childhood street address or even a teacher from the first grade but not to remember what she or he had for breakfast that same day. The patient may become lost a mile or two from home or may regress to his or her native language, spoken as a child, even though it may not have been spoken for many years. The next target for damage is the brain cortex, that part of the brain that serves a range of motor and sensory functions, including cognitive functions such as carrying on a conversation and motor functions such as walking. The degenerative process is widespread and may affect various areas of the cortex at random. Parts of the brainstem may be involved in this destructive process, which can cause faulty swallowing. Food can be aspirated into the lungs resulting in pneumonia. Hallucinations and paranoia can also occur. The ability to walk, read, speak, and recognize family may ultimately be lost.

Alzheimer support groups have been helpful for family caregivers as the stresses seem never to end. At the advanced stage of deterioration, families seem to be able to accept the need for nursing home placement much better. How sad it is to see a formerly charming, lovable, beautiful, caring, and intelligent individual reduced to this state of existence. I dare say that dealing with Alzheimer's is one of life's most difficult situations, and very few families are spared such suffering.

About a dozen new drugs have been developed over the past decade that may be effective in treating the symptoms of Alzheimers.[3] Acetylcholine (ACH) is needed in the brain for preserving memory. Cholinesterase is an enzyme that breaks down acetylcholine. Medications are being developed that prevent this reaction from occurring. One such drug is Tacrine (Cognex); it is available, expensive, and has some untoward side effects such as liver toxicity. Investigators are still working for improved medications. Another approach is to increase acetylcholine secretion in the brain. Linoprin is a drug with these properties; it releases acetylcholine as well as other enzymes needed to transmit messages within the brain. Other drugs being developed attempt to prevent the nerve cells from absorbing too much calcium. When excess calcium is deposited into the brain cells, they die. New calcium-blocker drugs, including Nimodipine, are being studied. The ultimate treatment for Alzheimer's disease—thus far not possible—would be a drug that blocked the depositing of amyloid in the brain cells. Alzheimer research continues. Using genetic engineering techniques, researchers can now breed strains of rats that congenitally develop the disease. This development presents new opportunities for further research.

The cost for nursing-home care continues to climb—some estimate as high as $30,000 a year per patient. It has been further estimated by the National Institute on Aging that keeping 10 percent of all Alzheimer patients out of nursing homes for one year would save about $9 billion.[4] Though nursing-home patients can become violent and confused, one must carefully consider when sedatives or even restraints are needed, and if there is a danger of the patient harming him- or herself or others. A patient's family may be unable to care for their sick loved ones adequately. Thus the family is faced with the progressively difficult situation of determining what truly is in the family and the patient's best interests. Besides Alzheimer support groups, there are respite programs that enable family caregivers at home to escape from the stress for a few weeks. The patient is cared for in a nursing facility while the caregiver is away.

In an attempt to educate medical students to the illnesses of the ever-growing elderly population, some medical schools, including Duke Medical School, have devised "The Aging Game," in which a roll of the dice determines, among other things, whether one becomes weaker, loses a prized possession, or wins praise for doing something right. In the game one can go from independent living status to nursing home just by a roll of the dice. Other medical schools have placed individual house officers (interns or residents) in a hospital bed and subjected each one to the same rules and restraints a real patient would endure. Both of these experiences seem to increase the sensitivities of future caregivers. Lectures may be forgotten, but balancing on a bedpan for the first time has a way of leaving an indelible impression.

As we get older, we all wonder if we, too, are not getting a bit forgetful. I know my spouse has said more than once that she had already told me about some event that seemed to be news to me. Many patients have told me about rare occasions when they have started to drive to town and then questioned themselves about the purpose of the trip, temporarily forgetting what they were supposed to accomplish. They, too, worry about senility. In a study relating self-evaluation of memory loss in healthy adults (ages thirty-nine to eighty-nine) to clinical memory tests, Dr. Karen I. Bolla and colleagues at the Johns Hopkins School of Medicine found that the self-rated memory disturbances reported by the subjects were more related to a depressed mood than to memory test performance.[5] Likewise, there is some evidence that depressed elderly are more likely to suffer chronic pain.[6] Such pain can be all-consuming, leaving little left to remember except the length of time that has passed since the last pain pill. Depression can often result in a failure to concentrate and an inability to think. Older people often encounter a problem when they compare their current memory to the memory they remember having when they were younger rather than comparing it to the memory of people the same age. Of course, there can be other pathologic causes for memory failure (metabolic disturbances, central nervous system illnesses, anemia, medications, for example); all such problems should be looked into by the family internist.

Theodore R. Bashore, of the Medical College of Pennsylvania, in a study on age and fitness, found that regular aerobic exercise may have, in addition to the benefits described earlier, a favorable effect on the central nervous system. The exercising group demonstrated an improved ability to process information when compared to the sedentary subjects. In other words, the decline of certain higher brain processes generally associated with aging may be reduced in people who exercise regularly.[7] R. E. Dustman and co-workers from Salt Lake City also noted that a sedentary lifestyle could be an important factor in promoting deterioration of both the physiological and thinking functions during the "normal aging process."[8] More research needs to be done in this area, yet the belief that regular exercise is the long sought after fountain of youth seems to be further strengthened by these studies.

Depression in the Elderly

The largest number of major depressions in the elderly are relapses from previous bouts of depression.[9] However, perhaps 15 percent of major depressions begin after age sixty. It is all too easy to attribute depression in the elderly to a physical ailment, a specific social change, or an economic issue and hence miss the depression itself. This misdiagnosis can lead to needless loss of quality of life and even suicide. Statistics show that 25 percent of all suicides are over sixty-five. As persons over sixty-five compose nearly 13 percent of the population this is a considerable and frightening problem.

Although people now are more open to recognizing depression and seeking treatment and are less reluctant to discuss it with others, the elderly still seem to hold on to the myth that it is a sign of weakness. The "I can lick it myself" or "I don't need a psychiatrist" attitude prevails. In nursing homes, 20 to 40 percent are very depressed according to Dr. Ari Kiev at New York City Payne Whitney Psychiatric Clinic.[10] Because so many changes occur as one gets older—changes that demand adjustments from the patient and the family—it is easy to see why the diagnosis of depression can be missed.

Young people, family, friends, and health-care providers may all feel that the elderly are supposed to be sad, and thereby not pick up on a potentially serious depression. This is all the more difficult in that the patient may not complain about any particular symptom but just "feel bad all over," or not be sleeping well, have lost his or her appetite, feel useless, feel aches and pains that fail to respond to treatment, experience weight loss, or exhibit a lack of energy. Those who care for the individual expect one to be "down in the dumps" when one's friends are dying, when one is concerned about being a burden to others in the family, and when one has worries about finances, potential loss of independence, and any number of acute or chronic medical conditions. Thus, a major depression can be missed, as it seems logical to consider these symptoms "normal" for the elderly.

Physicians try to meet the patient's physical needs such as good nutrition, exercise, and rest, but mental, emotional, and spiritual needs also must be addressed. Some signs found in depression such as memory loss may be attributed to Alzheimer's disease, and a patient could be mistakenly diagnosed as being senile. The patient could also present a mix of Alzheimer's disease and depression. Hobbies, social functions, and other activities can help the older person keep his or her mind sharp. The family, support groups, social workers, and the family doctor can all be emotional resources for an elderly person. The spirituality of the individual can be encouraged by being active in church, synagogue, or other place of worship. Cancer patients who have a strong spirituality generally have less anxiety than those who do not. Participation in a formal support group has also prolonged the lives of some cancer patients. Fifty women with breast cancer who were part of a support group survived twice as long as their counterparts in a control group with the same diagnosis who did not join.[11]

For those living home alone who may be aged or infirm, a device is now available that connects the individual to a response center via an "alarm button." The button can be worn around the neck or wrist and contains a cellular phone–type device that directly connects the patient to the response center. A push of the button notifies the center of the problem via the user's telephone line. A trained responder then asks what form of assistance is needed and promptly dispatches an ambulance, police, or fire engine depending on the nature of the call. If no response is received, the response center sends a police officer, neighbor, nurse, or some other predetermined person to the caller's address. Such technology may reduce the need for twenty-four–hour nursing care at home and possibly defer nursing home placement altogether. It also reassures family members.

Mercer County, New Jersey, has joined a network of trained volunteers, called "Reassurance Contact," who daily telephone elderly and handicapped clients who live alone. Reassurance Contact has been in continuous operation since 1976, and there are over 100 such agencies in the U.S. Trained volunteers call at the same prearranged time each day, and, if the call is not answered, help is sent immediately. There is no cost, and the same volunteer makes the daily call unless he or she is away, in which case a substitute volunteer takes over the duty. The client must notify the contact if he or she will not be home at the usual call time. Reassurance Contact's services include a crisis hotline, a suicide hotline, a support line, a telephone relay for the deaf, a reassurance line for the homebound, and information and referral services. A deaf person can also talk on the phone using a teletype through the service. The message is sent over telephone lines to a receiver that prints out the message. Some telephone companies have been providing similar services since the early 1980s.

Depression can be alleviated in many cases by using a combination of psychotherapy and medication. Prozac and Paxil are among the newer antidepressants that are effective and, overall, are well tolerated by the elderly. But even simple acts of caring can be very effective in brightening up the day of a person suffering from depression or Alzheimer's. There is something about a child, a pet, music, a group of young people, or even a teddy bear that warms the hearts of the elderly who are housebound or in a nursing home. I remember many times when I took one of my children on a house call to an elderly patient or to patients in the hospital. What a joy it would bring; the patient would often talk about it for many months.

The trick about depression is to detect it; the depressed patient will often deny being depressed and will often not want to take any medicine or seek therapy. Many of the current elderly are of a generation that viewed dependence on psychoactive medication or psychotheraphy as weakness. Those at greatest risk for suicide among the aged are elderly men, divorced or single, and the alcoholic elderly, according to Dr. Laurence J. Robbins, chief of geriatrics at the V.A. Center in Denver.[12] Patients in my office, obviously depressed, tears flowing down their cheeks have remarked, "I can make it alone; I don't need any medicine."

> My child, help your father in his old age,
> and do not grieve him as long as he lives;
>
> even if his mind fails, be patient with him;
> because you have all your faculties do not
> despise him.
>
> For kindness to a father will not be forgotten,
> and will be credited to you against your sins;
>
> in the day of your distress it will be remembered
>   in your favor;
> like frost in fair weather, your sins will melt away.
>   –Sirach 3:12–15

14

Repairing the Body Temple

The Cardiovascular System

B alloon angioplasty, now a well-established alternative for treating coronary artery disease, consists of dilating the body's cholesterol-filled arteries. If the arteries are unobstructed three to six months following the procedure, it is likely that the dilated artery will remain open for many months, even years. Of course, the lifestyle of the patient must be the best possible to keep the arteries free from the reaccumulation of cholesterol deposits.

Regression of Coronary Artery Disease

Jim is a remarkable seventy-year-old farmer who loved to ski at high altitudes. His heart condition had been treated many times since he turned sixty in order to allow him to work and play at full capacity. Jim had undergone two separate coronary by-pass operations and a subsequent balloon angioplasty of his diseased coronary artery grafts. Despite these treatments, he noted increasing chest pains once again. He even was unable to walk to the end of his 50-foot driveway without symptoms of chest discomfort. Jim was already taking the maximum amount of medication for his condition. It came to the point that there was not much more to do for this man.

He no longer smoked and was following a low-cholesterol diet, yet he continued to have chest pain. The surgeons were unwilling to try a third coronary by-pass operation.

Recent clinical research has demonstrated that reducing the serum cholesterol to below 100 mg. % can promote reabsorption of the cholesterol deposits obstructing the vessels.[1] Jim started taking a number of the approved medications to reduce his cholesterol level in 1989. After many months his cholesterol was brought down below 100 mg. %, and, soon after this, his angina disappeared, although he had not changed his cardiac medication. For the first time in many months, he was able to walk the length of the driveway and back without any chest pain. He was not, however, enthusiastic about undergoing yet another cardiac catheterization to prove that the arteries had reopened. We presumed that the cholesterol deposits were gone or greatly reduced. A stress test showed improvement in exercise capacity, but a repeat X-ray of his coronary arteries would have been the best way to determinate accurately their condition.

An increasing number of cases like Jim's are being reported. Dropping the blood cholesterol levels to very low numbers has promoted the reduction of cholesterol blockages; such reduction correlates with an improvement in symptoms. In some instances, repeat studies of the coronary arteries have demonstrated significant reduction in cholesterol deposits. Dr. Greg Brown at the University of Washington in Seattle studied two groups of patients with high blood cholesterol. Members of the first group were treated with diet alone, and members of the second group were treated with diet and an intensive use of lipid-lowering drugs. All subjects in the study were at high risk for a myocardial infarction. Of those in the diet-alone group, 46 percent demonstrated progression of disease; 11 percent showed regression over a two-and-one-half-year follow-up period. On the other hand, of those in the drug-treated group, progression of coronary disease was reduced by 50 percent, the regression rate was tripled, and the incidence of serious cardiac events was reduced by 73 percent.[2]

An additional finding reported in Brown's study was that those in the drug-treated group who had undergone coronary artery ballooning had less restenosis (return of blockage) than those treated by diet alone. Dr. John P. Kane and his co-workers at the University of California in San Francisco have noted regression of coronary lesions using combined drug therapy.[3] This development is very exciting and is on the cutting edge in coronary disease research since it may even diminish the need for open-heart surgery in some cases. Time will tell if this is possible, but it cautions us to measure the cholesterol levels of all preadolescents in order to prevent cholesterol build-up. Prevention still is the best treatment.

Other advances in the field of coronary disease treatment consist of using a diamond-studded rotoblator rotating at speeds of 190,000 rpm to clean out the clogged arteries. Drs. David Warth and Bert Green in Seattle are among the pioneers of this method.[4]

Laser treatment has some promise, but by 1993 it still hadn't really caught on in the U.S. and it remains in the investigational stages. Perhaps the technique will improve enough to be more widely employed in the near future.

Cardiac Transplantation

Cardiac transplantation is now an established procedure. By 1990, an estimated 12,600 heart transplants were performed according to the International Society for Heart Transplantation Registry. The real problem with heart transplantation is not the procedure, but the long wait for the scarce donor heart. There were an estimated 3,000 heart transplant candidates waiting in 1992, but no more than 2,000 donor hearts actually available. Evidence indicates those patients who were the sickest ("urgent" candidates) responded better to the surgery than those less sick ("regular" candidates). Lynne W. Stevenson, an American Heart Association researcher, found that 75 percent of the urgent candidates survived compared to 60 percent of the regular candidates.[5] She found that despite the higher operative risk in the urgent cases, such a slightly higher risk was relatively minor compared to the high risk of not performing the heart transplantation at all.

Much of the need for heart transplants stems from the fact that patients who survive heart attacks or other conditions damaging the heart (some viral diseases, for example) develop enlarged and poorly functioning hearts, which can lead to chronic heart failure. Many such patients cannot be helped by cardiac drugs and treatments and become virtually bedridden. An estimated 400,000 new cases of heart failure arise every year. Chief cardiac surgeon Keith Reemtsma of Columbia-Presbyterian Hospital in New York stated that 90 percent of his patients go back to work or school following heart transplant surgery; 70 percent survived five years without further surgery. Almost all of these patients would have died from heart failure within a year without the transplant.[6]

Two new developments may increase the heart-donor pool. The first is the ability to extend the life of the donor organ from a few hours to up to fourteen hours, as the result of a new organ-preserving solution that increases the length of time the heart can be preserved outside of the donor. This development might increase the heart-donor pool by 30 percent, enabling hospitals to transport organs from remote areas. Cardiac surgeons would also have more time to prepare the operating room and assemble the staff. The second factor is the realization that the body weight of the donor need not be similar to the body weight of the recipient. The size of a harvested heart doesn't always correlate with the body size of the recipient. Echocardiograms (heart dimensions obtained by sound waves) play an important role in this matching process and are actually more accurate than comparisons of body weight.[7] One of my huskier male patients is doing very well with a donor heart from a small woman, for example.

Hospitals have certain criteria for selecting transplantation candidates. The Henry Ford Hospital lists three basic prerequisites:

1. The patient must suffer from severe heart disease, have a poor one-year prognosis despite maximal medical and surgical treatment, and be otherwise healthy;
2. The patient may be no older than sixty-five;
3. The patient must be motivated and psychologically stable and have good family support.[8]

Heart Transplant: A Second Chance

Harry is a fifty-five-year-old stockbroker who developed a bacterial infection on his mitral valve and in addition suffered from severe coronary artery disease. Despite mitral valve repair and coronary artery by-pass surgery, his condition gradually deteriorated. Over a period of two to three years, he began to experience progressively more frequent bouts of heart failure. As his heart gradually enlarged, he developed progressive mitral valve leakage and his shortness of breath become more severe. Ultimately, he became bedridden. Even this low level of activity failed to halt his heart's downhill course, and he eventually reached the point of requiring constant intravenous medications to keep his blood pressure from falling too low. His kidneys were also slowing down because of his deteriorating cardiac condition. He remained bedridden and required constant intravenous medications for nine months while waiting for a donor heart. At last the day arrived! The operation was performed at a large metropolitan hospital. His routine follow-up was rigorous, with frequent tests, biopsies, and examinations as well as chemotherapy and the use of cortisone. I could detect a slow but steady improvement as the weeks rolled by. Now, one year after his new heart, Harry can miraculously walk two miles a day. His signs of heart failure have vanished. He feels very thankful as does his family. Harry asserts that the least he can do now is to give talks at forums highlighting the need for more donor hearts and other organs. As he shares his life in these talks, his message is especially strong because he is living proof of the importance of a second chance. His mind, body, and spirit have been uplifted.

After receiving a heart transplant, Robert G. Clouse, professor of history at Indiana State University in Terre Haute, Indiana, reflected, "Getting up in the morning is special. Every once in a while I pull off the shelf a book that's been waiting a long time, crack it open, and realize I almost didn't get to read this one." Understandably, he appreciates the joy of being active again. He is deeply sensitive to the complex decisions that must be made in choosing any recipient for an organ transplant. He remarked that, although the biomedical advances of the past three decades continue to give many ethical headaches,

headaches are not the only things they bring; it's the second chance to live again that is so wonderful, and Robert Clouse feels very blessed.[9] Brother David Steindl-Rast expresses this sentiment well, "For happiness is not what makes us grateful. It is gratefulness that makes us happy."[10] Being thankful for our blessings gives us an inner joy. Too often in our daily rushing about, we don't quiet ourselves long enough to appreciate the good things that we have or the providential outcomes of what seemed to be dark periods in our lives. The more we are thankful, the more we recognize the work of God's grace. Giving praise and being thankful, like turning on a water faucet, open the way for God to shower us with even more of his bounteous gifts. Harry's heart is once again strong; he is thankful for this second chance. His message is powerful; his credentials are unbeatable!

> In my distress I called upon the Lord;
> to my God I cried for help.
> From his temple he heard my voice,
> and my cry to him reached his ears.
> –Psalm 18:6

Coronary artery disease in the transplanted heart is the main cause of death after the operation, and how to prevent recurrence of the disease is a subject of constant investigation. Physicians caring for large numbers of these patients agree that chest pain typical of angina rarely occurs. This lack of pain is thought to be caused by the denervation of the transplanted heart; that is, the nerves that would normally transmit the pain of angina were eliminated during surgery.

Cardiomyoplasty

Chronic heart failure is becoming increasingly more common in the U.S. People are living longer because of newer medications and advances in bioengineering such as prosthetic heart valves and implantable defibrillators such as pacemakers. After years of chronic heart failure the time often comes when the patient is barely alive, at the end of the line, and something must be done. Donor hearts are in short supply, so transplantation is often not possible. One alternative is cardiomyoplasty. Currently five centers in the United States are authorized to carry out cardiomyoplasty. In this surgical procedure the patient's own latissimus dorsi muscle (located by the wingbone or scapula) is wrapped around the failing heart muscle, providing a mechanical assistance to the heart. A specialized pacemaker is attached to the latissimus muscle. This stimulates the latissimus so that it contracts simultaneously with the heart. By June 1991, over 100 patients had undergone this type of surgery. Cardiomyoplasty has some advantages over heart transplantation: there is no need for chemotherapy and cortisone to prevent organ rejection nor is there a need for multiple heart biopsies of the inner heart lining. Also, unlike a heart transplantation, since the transplanted tissue comes from the patient him- or herself, there is no problem with the immune system. The patient's congestive heart failure improves after the operation. The total cost for this procedure, along with the follow-up care, is much less than that of a heart transplantation. A large number of potential candidates already exist, and I'm sure the number will increase each year. The basic problem in chronic heart failure whether the result of toxins (such as alcohol), viral infection, or scarring from prior heart attacks is that the heart muscle is no longer able to efficiently push the blood around the body; it is a problem of "pump failure."

Divine Intervention for a Heart Attack Victim

Denny is a seventy-one-year-old retired auto mechanic. While working in his backyard one Sunday afternoon, he collapsed. Denny had suffered a heart attack two years earlier, and a remaining small area of the scar tissue was responsible for inducing serious heart palpitations. After successful coronary by-pass surgery and partial removal of scar tissue from the damaged site following his first heart attack, the area inside the heart causing the dangerous rhythm disturbance was supposedly removed along with the scar tissue itself. Despite the surgery, he was suffering another cardiac arrest. At the very instant of Denny's fall an emergency medical technician (EMT) with the local rescue squad happened to be biking along in front of Denny's house and saw the whole thing. This was the first time the technician had biked in that part of town. The EMT jumped off his bike and ran across the grass to where Denny lay motionless, unresponsive, inert. He started CPR while a neighbor called the rescue squad. It just so happened that the Lifemobile was parked around the corner, sponsoring a plant sale to raise funds. (Lifemobiles are emergency-response vehicles equipped with a defibrillator, telephone communication with the hospital, and all the medications heart attack victims need. Lifemobiles, in operation in many cities and towns, are staffed mostly by trained volunteers.) In the Lifemobile, Denny was resuscitated from a lethal rhythm disturbance by receiving an electrical defibrillation shock to the chest. He was hospitalized and did well except for bursts of ventricular tachycardia (bursts of rapid and dangerous heart rhythms), for which he received constant intravenous medication. Further studies at a large university medical center revealed that no drugs could effectively control the life-threatening rhythm disturbance to Denny's heart. What finally did work was a defibrillator implanted in his heart that would automatically deliver a low-voltage electrical shock (which is not felt by the patient) whenever the pacemaker detected the onset of the lethal rhythm. Denny has done very well now for the past two years. After two separate open heart surgeries, his life seems to have turned around, and, after many years of being scolded, he finally stopped smoking!

Denny's case illustrates another advance in bioengineering, but, it also presents, I believe, an example of divine intervention. The EMT, who had never been in that part of town before and was trained in resuscitative techniques, just happened to cycle by at the right time; the Lifemobile just happened to be around the corner. So many times the Lord intervenes on our behalf. One might call these instances lucky or coincidental, but I know they aren't. The following by Marion Noll, O.S.U., appies to Denny's true story:

> Jesus' words brought Thomas to faith; we too, can hear Jesus speak to us, not directly, but through the people he sends into our lives.[11]

Other Medical Advances
to Preserve the Body Temple

Various other organs are now being successfully transplanted. In 1990, there were 17,938 kidney transplants, 1,794 heart transplants, 1,242 liver transplants, 473 pancreatic transplants, 309 lung transplants, and 226 combination heart-lung transplants.[12] Additional body parts that can be transplanted include the cornea, bone, skin, and heart valves.

Many other advances are occurring in other areas of medicine as well. Endoscopic surgery (surgery using a device to look inside a hollow organ without cutting it open) is now a routine option in many cases and is now used for removal of organs. This procedure is less invasive and results in less cost, shorter hospital stay, and a quicker return to work. Small electrical parts are being developed that will help restore some dexterity to damaged extremities. Workers at the National Institutes of Health (NIH) are working on new cloning techniques whereby the body can be aided in rebuilding its own tendons, ligaments, bone, and cartilage. This method, if successful, would send the field of orthopedics in an entirely new direction. The seemingly impossible task of implanting brain cells as a treatment for Parkinson's and Alzheimer's diseases is also being studied.

Research is underway to develop ways to assist the immune system. Our immune system weakens somewhat as we age, but should the system break down as it does with AIDS, then organisms such as bacteria or viruses can overwhelm the body, resulting in critical illness or death. As the body ages, it may not be able to distinguish between normal and abnormal tissues. Under such conditions antibodies may mobilize against normal tissues instead of fighting the abnormal "invaders." When antibodies are formed against normal organs or tissues, autoantibodies are created, which can destroy normal tissues. In diabetes (adult-onset, noninsulin type), a form of antibody called the "T-cell" attacks the normal insulin-making cells resulting in a shortage of insulin production by the body. Because of this, work is underway to transplant insulin cells into the body. Monoclonal antibodies (antibodies composed of a single cell) are being developed that will recognize certain cancers and attach to them. It is hoped that anticancer drugs will be able to use these antibodies to locate and destroy malignant cells.

Research is also ongoing into less health-threatening but often undesired conditions. Hair transplantation using hair from the same patient and the drug minoxidil are being used to treat baldness. Unfortunately, once minoxidil treatment is stopped, the hair apparently becomes sparse again.

The list of medical advances is unending. Space doesn't allow for all the discoveries that are taking place. The future of medicine will be greatly influenced by further bioengineering developments as well as by genetic engineering. More will be said about genetic engineering in the following chapter.

15

Genetic Engineering

Gene Therapy

M olecular genetics, or gene therapy, is a medical revolution that according to Dr. Leroy Hood of the California Institute of Technology "will change medicine more in the next 20 years than it has been in the past 2,000."[1] The hope and expectation for the practice of medicine is the promotion of the body's ability to make its own "medicine" rather than relying on drugs and procedures. One of the projects being studied by Dr. Steven Rosenberg, Dr. Marston Linehan, and others at the NIH concerns using genetic engineering to try to cure malignant melanoma, a deadly skin cancer that kills 30,000 Americans a year. A gene exists in all human cells that produces a strong anticancer protein called TNF (tumor necrosis factor). Unfortunately, the body does not make enough of this protein to eradicate tumors. One approach to treating melanoma consists of first isolating 100 million cells extracted from the malignant melanoma tumor. These cells, called TILs (tumor infiltrating lymphocytes), are modified to carry TNF through special genetic engineering techniques. Next, the cells are injected back into the patient. The injected cells find their way to the cancer cells, release the TNF once they are inside the tumors, and kill the cancer on the spot. This procedure, still in the research phase, illustrates one approach to curing cancer through gene therapy.

Another approach being studied is called monoclonal therapy. In this procedure a strong chemotherapy drug is combined with an antibody protein that hones in on an antigen found on the surface of tumor cells. When the antibody with its attached chemotherapeutic drug contacts the surface antigen of the cancer cell, it is drawn inside the tumor. The drug is then released, killing the tumor cell by destroying the tumor cell's chromosomes. This therapy produced a 70 percent cure rate in mice in which human breast, colon, and lung tumor cells had been implanted.

Cloning is a method of making unlimited numbers of a particular segment of deoxyribonucleic acid (DNA), the essential building block of life. The process of cloning starts with a circular unit of DNA obtained from bacterial cells. Certain enzymes are employed to break both the circular DNA from bacteria as well as the circular segment of genomic DNA. The genomic DNA is spliced to bacteria-produced DNA, closing a broken circle and resulting in a recombined DNA molecule. Recombinant molecules are then introduced inside of bacterial cells (E. Coli). These bacteria multiply and start producing the protein coded by the recombinant gene. The recombinant DNA can then be extracted from the protein and used in research.

Dr. Ira Pastan, a primary investigator of the National Cancer Institute, has recently reported that many cancers overproduce growth-factor receptors located within the abnormal cells. These growth-factor receptors can be coded by using bacterial genes and DNA fusion. A special protein is then produced to selectively kill those cancer cells with the same growth-factor receptors. Hence, cancer toxins can be produced. There are a number of such toxins now under scrutiny. The bacterium *Pseudomonas,* for example, produces a toxin that can be genetically engineered to attack cancers of the colon, breast, and prostate. Such toxins will be a powerful tool in the treatment of the metastatic cancer that remains after surgery, standard chemotherapy, or radiation therapy.[2]

Dr. Ronald Levy of Stanford University has succeeded in developing a vaccine for the recurrence of B-cell lymphoma using genetic engineering techniques that stimulate a patient's immune system. The vaccine is grown from the patient's own tumors and, thus, is custom-made for each patient.[3] He stresses that this procedure is not designed to protect people from getting the cancer in the first place but rather to prevent recurrence of the cancer in patients who are in complete remission by stimulating the immune system against a specific type of tumor. Researchers hope that they will be able to treat many types of cancer with such genetic engineering techniques.

The application of genetic engineering to other diseases is being studied as well. The gene defect for cystic fibrosis was detected in lab cultures in 1990, and it is hoped that treatment for correcting the disease will be available within the next several years. In addition to cystic fibrosis, through genetic research physicians can now test for Tay-Sachs disease, sickle-cell anemia, Down syndrome, Duchenne muscular dystrophy, neurofibromatosis, and retinoblastoma. Other advances in disease detection include a test for the abnormal "Philadelphia" chromosome responsible for chronic myelogenous leukemia. This test provides the physician with a new ability to monitor the course of treatment. Cures for some diseases may be developed in which physicians actually replace the patient's defective gene with its normal counterpart.

Although much is being done regarding gene isolation, the majority of diseases caused by inherited defective genes are not treatable employing gene therapy. By using animal models, defects similar to human diseases can be created. These animals in turn can be used for gene treatment experiments before applying the techniques to humans. It is hoped that with further technological advances permanent correction of genetic defects will be possible.

The human cell is composed of about 100,000 different genes; these genes regulate the production of the proteins that are vital to the structure and function of all the cells in the body. The genes are located on twenty-three pairs of chromosomes, which are present in virtually every cell of the body. If even one of the pairs of chromosomes goes astray, a genetic defect occurs (an abnormality in chromosome 21 causes Down syndrome, for example).

James Watson and Francis Crick discovered the structure of DNA in 1953, which was probably the start of modern-day genetics. The federal government has allotted $3 billion over the next fifteen years to aid in further DNA research; the grant is called the Human Genome Project. The object of the HGP is to identify every human gene. Already more than 1,800 genes have been isolated (such as the genes responsible for sickle-cell anemia and Tay-Sachs disease). DNA-based tests can, for example, identify the precise cause of a given pneumonia when other tests cannot.

Other by-products of genetic engineering include hepatitis B vaccine, human insulin, influenza vaccines, and human growth hormone. DNA-markers can be used to identify Huntington's disease and genetic defects in low density cho-lesterol (LDL) metabolism. As mentioned earlier, LDL is a major "bad guy" in heart disease. Determining the genetic defect that causes a given disease can greatly assist in the dis-ease's treatment and prevention. However, a word of caution—the strictest confidence must be maintained when examining the genetic composition of a patient because, as genetic engineering techniques advance, employers and insur-ance companies may exploit this information.

The field of medical ethics will increasingly be tested as genetic research and treatment develops. For example, as congenital defects are detected in fetuses prior to delivery and as genetic defects are found that can lead to serious illnesses in midlife, society must decide what course of action to take. Questions raised in a lecture by Dr. Eric Lander, chief of the Human Genome Project at M.I.T., concerned the issue of a pregnant woman carrying to term a fetus that was expected to die within a month after delivery from a fatal disease called spinal muscular atrophy.[4] Such questions have enormous ram-ifications when considering that, to date, science has already been able to localize 100 inherited diseases on human chro-mosomes. The advantage of identifying these diseases is to be able to find individuals early on who, for example, carry the gene for cancer of the colon and to then follow them closely with colonoscopy at regular intervals. Genes have been dis-covered that are responsible for several hundred genetic dis-eases. Besides myotonic dystrophy, others include cystic fibrosis, fragile X syndrome, amyotrophic lateral sclerosis (ALS, or Lou Gehrig's disease), and Down syndrome. Once a gene is isolated and mutations are noted, one is able to test an individual to see if he or she is a "carrier." Thirty thousand people in the U.S. have cystic fibrosis, but it is estimated that twelve million people carry the defective gene. Since a child must inherit two defective genes in order to have the disease, molecular genetics may play a significant role in family planning if both potential parents test positive. Reducing humans to a series of genes that can potentially be engineered or eliminated, or changed, comes close to interfering with the Lord's work. Great care must be taken in using genetic engineering tools. These tools may be wonderful if used to remove harmful genes from the body, but not if they are used "eugenically" to build a "master race," as Hitler tried to do during World War II.

As early as 1982, Pope John Paul II proclaimed that "the research of modern biology gives hope that the transfer and mutation of genes can ameliorate the condition of those who are affected by chromosomic diseases."[5] In 1986, the National Council of Churches issued a document supporting genetic screening as a way to eliminate harmful genes from the gene pool.[6] It seems, therefore, that the benefits of genetic engineering far outweighs the possible drawbacks. All of us must take part in the ethical decisions that are made as scientific advances continue. It would be wise to create a national policy resource center to address the ethical, legal, and social implications of this field. Some kind of policy should be in place, for example, before more and more tests for predisposition to colon cancer, breast cancer, Alzheimer's disease, and other conditions are developed rather than after the tests are already in use. Nevertheless, the possibility that the Genome Project and similar projects around the globe will better the human condition are excellent.

Dr. Leroy Hood claims that the Genome Project will lead to a detailed micropharmacology of cells. "We rationally will design drugs to be targeted to the particular protein that we know is effective in a particular case and to help it carry out its function or prevent it from killing a cell."[7] This development bodes well for all.

Genetics, New Therapy, and a Heart Attack Victim

George, a sixty-one-year-old car salesman, came to the emergency room at 5 a.m. complaining of severe chest pain across his chest and radiating down both arms and into the jaw. He had recovered quite well from a heart attack several years previously and recognized this pattern of discomfort to be the same as he had experienced then. (I usually tell a patient at the time of a heart attack that the distress he or she is experiencing would henceforth be known as his or her "signature.") He said this was a return of his "signature." His electrocardiogram revealed an acute injury in an area of the heart different from the previous site. George was an appropriate patient for intravenous tissue plasminogen activator (TPA) therapy, which was administered after the interim history, physical examination, and all the necessary laboratory tests were conducted. Plasminogen, a substance found in the blood, is a precursor to plasmin, a proteolytic enzyme that dissolves the fibrin blood clot. The conversion of plasminogen to plasmin is carried out by special enzymes: tissue plasminogen activator (TPA) and streptokinase. Fortunately, George's response to treatment was typical, and he showed a significant relief of chest pain, a less acute response on the electrocardiogram, a burst of ventricular heart rhythm abnormalities (suggesting the opening up of a closed, or thrombotic, coronary artery), and an improvement of his blood pressure. Subsequent cardiac catheterization many days later revealed some new areas of damage but probably far less than might have developed had the enzyme (TPA) not been given.

George's case illustrates the benefit genetic engineering has had on the treatment of heart attack patients. A number of the agents are now available, including streptokinase, and many studies are underway to determine the advantages of each enzyme. Coronary thrombosis is found in the large majority of patients whose coronary arteries are studied within four hours after the onset of heart attack symptoms. If the blocked coronary artery can be opened within six hours (preferably sooner if possible), there is good evidence that the amount of damage to the ventricle will be significantly less, complications (such as heart failure and rhythm disturbances) will be minimized, and mortality will be reduced. One such product is manufactured under the name Activase. The active enzyme is alteplase, a TPA. Large quantities of alteplase can be obtained through genetic engineering techniques. Alteplase is synthesized using DNA from human melanoma cells. Manufacturing the alteplase consists of collecting the alteplase that is secreted in a mamallian cell culture (such as Chinese hamster ovary cells) into which the DNA has been inserted.[8] The resulting product is called TPA (recombinant TPA).

A new world is opening up in the field of genetic engineering, and Activase is only one example of genetic engineering products that are employed in most hospitals today. There are other ways of manufacturing proteins for human use. For example, a bacterium is often used to act as a "factory" to make human proteins in large amounts and inexpensively. DNA is like a blueprint for producing a certain sequence of proteins. To create such a sequence one obtains a copy of the DNA of the particular protein to be produced, and the DNA is then inserted into the bacterium, where it multiplies within the cell. The new artificially made human protein can then be removed (harvested) from the bacterial cells. A number of human proteins can be created using such new technology. Research employing this procedure includes work on vaccines for AIDS, tuberculosis, leprosy, typhoid as well as studies on producing albumin and diagnosing various viruses in body tissues.[9]

In September 1992, gene therapy for non–small-cell carcinoma of the lung was approved for human studies for the first time. In this therapy, the surgeon first removes as much of the tumor as possible. The genetic composition of the excised tumor is then determined; two of the genes commonly found in such tumors are the "K-ras gene" and the "p53 gene." To treat the K-ras type tumor a harmless "mirror image" gene is attached to a similarly harmless virus. This substance is then injected into the patient's lungs using a bronchoscope. The harmless virus destroys the cancer cells leaving the normal cells alone. Researchers hope that tumor cells will thus shrink and disappear. A slightly different therapy treats the p53 gene, but the genetic engineering principles are the same.[10]

Dr. Leroy Hood described a method used successfully in mice and to be considered soon in humans as a way to eliminate genetic disorders from a family. If a woman carries a genetic disease, such as Huntington's chorea, and wants a baby, she is fertilized through in vitro fertilization. Several of her eggs are placed in a test tube along with her husband's sperm and become fertilized. After searching among the fertilized eggs, the one without the Huntington's genetic defect is then implanted in the womb. The baby would then be healthy at birth, the family free of the deadly gene, and the couple would not face the difficult choice of aborting an afflicted fetus, as it would not be transmitted to subsequent generations.[11]

The exciting world of genetic engineering is just beginning. Despite the serious ethical questions raised by new medical technologies, research into this area must continue. We know that the Lord wants his children to be whole and to be healthy and one cannot help but believe that genetic engineering research is in keeping with his plan for each of us.

Further Reading

Leon Jaroff, *The New Genetics: The Human Genome Project and Its Impact on the Practice of Medicine* (Knoxville, Tenn.: Whittle Direct Books, 1991).

An excellent book written in a manner that physicians with a limited knowledge in the fast-moving field of genetics as well as interested lay people will find informative. It describes the ongoing research to map the 100,000 genes that are thought to be contained within each human cell. The project is expected to lead to the identification of genes that are responsible for specific diseases and thus allow physicians to predict which individuals are genetically predisposed to specific illnesses. This book offers a glimpse into the exciting new science of genetic engineering.

16

The End: Parting with the Body Temple

T om is a sixty-eight-year-old former private investigator who just returned from a trip to Russia, where he was doing consulting work. In many ways Tom is different from other men his age in that he is not yet retired, works daily, and is under treatment for diabetes, heart disease, and kidney disease. In addition, he has lost one leg because of poor circulation and is blind. Despite these liabilities, he has continued to contribute to society. He has been able to do so with the help of two things: much courage and a kidney transplant. When a patient reaches end-stage kidney failure, the only two options left are dialysis or kidney transplantation. Tom was fortunate to receive a kidney transplant. Sometimes, while awaiting a donor kidney, a patient must be kept alive for months by dialysis (a process wherein machines periodically flush the retained kidney excretions from the body).

Many patients wait for several years to receive a donor kidney. In 1987 in New Jersey alone, 350 patients were waiting for a suitable donor kidney; over 17,000 were waiting nationally.[1] Although 75 percent of Americans are willing to donate their organs for transplantation, not enough attention is paid to organ donation when a family member is near death. In New Jersey there is a twenty-four–hour on-call Organ Procurement Team who will assist in the donating process, that is, review the case prior to death, aid in identifying the organ or organs that would be useful, help obtain the organ or tissue promptly after brain death occurs, coordinate the meeting of medical and legal requirements, institute tissue-typing procedures, and transport the donor organs swiftly to the awaiting transplant surgeon and patient. These duties require a great deal of teamwork. Before an organ is removed various tests are performed to confirm that the patient is brain-dead. Relatives must understand this before they can be approached for organ donation consent.

In 1991, 800 people in New Jersey alone were waiting for an organ transplant, and the list grows yearly. Susan Van Pelt is a transplant coordinator for New Jersey. She states that it is important when approaching relatives of a potential donor to assess at what point in the grieving process the family members find themselves: "Different families have different needs. Some families like to talk about the person, who they were." The coordinators also try to answer the family's questions about the organ transplant program and reassure the loved ones that the brain-dead patient will feel no pain. Organ donation is much easier if people discuss the matter beforehand with their family and fill out an organ donor card.

The shortage of donor organs is a multifaceted problem. In 1991, 24,797 patients were waiting for a variety of donor organs according to the nonprofit agency United Organ Network for Organ Sharing (UONOS). The same agency estimated that 2,200 people died in the U.S. in 1990 while waiting for an organ transplant.[2] Since the federal government often pays for the cost of kidney dialysis for patients with end-stage kidney disease, more donor kidneys could save $3.5 billion by reducing the number of patients on dialysis. Transplantation also results in an immense improvement in the quality of life for patients.

We physicians have all had patients who were given a second chance by receiving an organ. What joy this act brings to the living and what gratitude to the donor who died.

Generosity That Led to a New Life

In *A Physician's Witness,* I described Brad, a young university student who, without any warning, collapsed in his room unconscious. Upon arrival of professional help, many minutes had passed, and, although his heartbeat was restored to a normal rhythm, he was declared brain-dead. He never regained consciousness. Once this fact was accepted by all members of the health team and the family, his kidneys were successfully donated to another young person, Mark, whose life before the surgery had been anchored to a dialysis machine. The new life given helped to assuage the great grief we all felt. Prompt donation of a healthy organ may allow someone else to have a second chance for a better life.

Preparing for Death at Home or in the Hospital

We are fortunate to have a hospice program associated with our medical center. The purpose of the program is to allow the dying patient with less than six months to live to remain at home among caring family members and friends but at the same time to have the health team take an active part in the caring process.

There must, however, be a primary caregiver who lives in the home, such as a spouse or family member, in order for the patient to be eligible for the service. The patient must no longer be able to care for him- or herself.

The hospice has an overall supervisor who is responsible for the programs. There are, on any given day, seventeen to twenty patients enrolled in the program at our facility. A number of other health-care providers are also included in the service. The health aide is at the home daily and helps with bathing, feeding, dressing, toiletry, and so forth. The visiting nurse comes to the house at regular intervals and checks the patient's vital signs and reports changes to the physician. The family physician also may elect to visit from time to time to see firsthand how things are going and to review medications. A clergy member stops by, as needed, and ministers to the spiritual needs of the patient and (often) of the family. Social workers are also involved and handle the many administrative duties of running a program, offering support and help with equipment, therapists, oxygen requests, and so forth.

The hospice program has existed at our medical center for over fifteen years, and I can attest to the peace it contributes to both patient and family.

Sometimes the unexpected will happen, such as a sudden hemorrhage or other illness that will require a short-term emergency hospital stay. But once the problem is solved the patient goes back home to the program.

Frequently a single person who has no primary caregiver at home becomes very ill and dies in the hospital. This may take place over a matter of several days rather than several months as is often the case in hospice patients. Of course the health team are all there, but in a general hospital setting instead of a home setting. I remember a much-loved and respected music teacher who was gay and single and had no companion or family member at home who could act as a primary caregiver. He was dying from cancer. One of his former students flew up from the South to be with him. The former student stayed by his hospital bed day and night for several days, all the time quietly holding his hand, while his friend slowly died. It was one of the most touching and heartrending acts of love I've witnessed. The hospital can be a humane and compassionate environment for one's final days, especially when someone who deeply cares is present.

A living will can be an important part of preparing for death. It can help a terminally ill patient die with dignity. In a living will a person makes his or her wishes clear about such things as invasive treatments, ventilator treatment, and other life-preserving "heroic" measures. It is a great relief to health-care providers and to the family to know a patient's wishes on this matter. Under normal circumstances, should a patient suddenly become critically ill, nurses and physicians must do everything medically possible to keep the patient alive (no matter what quality of life that is) unless the living will has indicated otherwise. Today, private physicians and hospitals are making an effort to obtain living wills from their patients. In our hospital, a large supply of samples are available. Even if one is not sick it is worthwhile to consider one's attitude about life-preserving measures and about the end of life.

The Lord created human beings out of earth,
and makes them return to it again.

He gave them a fixed number of days,
but granted them authority over everything on the earth.

He endowed them with strength like his own,
and made them in his own image.

Discretion and tongue and eyes,
ears and a mind for thinking he gave them.

He filled them with knowledge and understanding,
and showed them good and evil.

Their eyes saw his glorious majesty,
and their ears heard the glory of his voice.

He said to them, "Beware of all evil."
And he gave commandment to each of them concerning
the neighbor.

–Sirach 17:1–3, 6–7, 13–14

Summary

T his book is about the human body—the body temple. The body temple consists of a trinity of mind, body, and spirit. We must care for this beautiful gift from our Lord. In order to be a whole person, all three components of the body temple must be integrated and work together in harmony. The interdependence of mind, body, and spirit has been recognized through the ages. Much has been written about these three parts in scripture, and it seems that in recent times the secular press has been devoting more coverage to the issues of a higher being and the spiritual dimension of each human being. The contemporary interest in spirituality may be a reflection of the world's searching for a deeper meaning of life, a life that is often fragmented, confusing, and complex. We need an anchor, a rock of strength, a hope for things eternal. Because job loss, illness, poverty, hunger, oppression, injustice, and greed are so rampant, we need to return "home"—a place of inner peace and inner healing, a prize beyond our grasp despite all our scientific progress and material successes. But this gem can only come from the grace of God, as a gift of the Holy Spirit. As each day comes to a close, we have one day less to build a better body temple from the pieces of our fragmented selves. It behooves each of us to take stock of our body temple, to acknowledge this gift we have received, and to cherish it for our own good as well as for the good of those around us.

This book is concerned with preserving, using, maintaining, repairing, replacing, and, at the close of life, donating parts of this wondrous body we have all been given. I have presented many true cases to illustrate these points. Some remarkable medical and surgical advances, all fruits of human ingenuity, have been described, and I have touched upon some of the newer medicines, procedures, and the new world of genetic engineering, which are all directed to the purpose of keeping our bodies whole. Despite all these advances, the health of our body temple boils down to the acknowledgment that our Lord's presence is the center point of all advances. It is his presence, the kingdom of God that is within, that will ultimately be the force that coordinates our wholeness. The way we respect our body temple tells the community at large how we respect our Lord. For, as Natalie Goldberg writes,

> We don't live for ourselves; we are interconnected. We live for the earth, for Texas, for the chicken we ate last night that gave us its life, for our mother, for the highway and the ceiling and the trees. We have a responsibility to treat ourselves kindly; then we will treat the world the same way.[1]

If we abuse our body temple, trash it, throw away this gift, not only will our lives reflect a disregard for goodness but our relationships with others will reflect this same disrespect. How one treats one's body has an impact on the body of society, the community of believers. We do not live in isolation from others.

By trying to live a God-centered life, we are more likely to be complete in mind, body, and spirit. Our body temple will then be functioning optimally as the years pass by, and we will have the necessary strength, courage, and inner peace to enjoy life and better serve others.

How does one cope with all the changes and challenges we face as we grow older? Often a team approach is needed. Each member of the team can contribute special knowledge and skills. Some of these helpers consist of physical therapists, occupational therapists, friends, family, clergy, and sports partners. Other avenues that uplift are literature, art, and music. Intergenerational involvement such as spending time with one's grandchildren, optimism, community involvement, and continued intellectual stimulation are important. A healthy lifestyle, which includes good nutrition, exercise, regular visits for medical care, and safety responsibility, is crucial. Faith in God and his plan is most important.

I have described individuals in their late teens, midlife, and old age who have been exposed to a multitude of challenges that have illustrated the importance and interdependence of the mind, body, and spirit. With the passing of the years, each of us has had (and will continue to have) challenges, some welcome and others not. With God's grace we can address these challenges and grow in spiritual strength. The concertmaster is the spiritual center, the Holy Spirit, who will direct us through each stage of life. But we have to listen daily and to trust his guidance. It is this same comforter that lifts us into eternal life at the time of death. The symphony of life relies on God's direction. The body parts may crumble, be restored, replaced, and may ultimately cease to function, but the spiritual center, the kingdom of God within, will continue forever. It is never too late, even after a life of abusing the body temple, to make a 180-degree turn. I have seen cases in which the individual's lifestyle changes, emotional stability and physical health improve, and an inner peace and spirituality develop. Such a change is like a resurrection, like a reconciliation. A peaceful death can result in a spiritual healing—the body dies yet the patient and those who are close and dear are healed.

I would like to end with the thoughts of French physician Jacques Sarano about the sanctity of the human body.

The body is the language that God has given to us in order to know him, to understand him or to reject him, to cooperate or to refuse to cooperate in the creation. And the body is also the means God uses to make all this known to us. It is the language from him to us and from us to him. This is why we have dared to say that the body is given to us as a sacrament.[2]

Notes

Introduction
1. Jacques Sarano, *The Meaning of the Body,* trans. James H. Farley (Philadelphia: Westminster Press, 1966), 16.
2. Paul Pierson, "The Easy Way," *Daily Word* 129, no. 1 (1991): 10.
3. Henri J. M. Nouwen, *Show Me the Way* (New York: Crossroad, 1992), 31.

Chapter 1: A Christian Physician's View of the Body Temple
1. *The Word among Us* 10, no. 4 (1991): 27.
2. Murray Bodo, O.F.M., *The Way of St. Francis* (New York: Image Books/Doubleday, 1984), 165.
3. Barbara Shlemon, *Healing the Hidden Self* (Notre Dame, Ind.: Ave Maria Press, 1982), 125.
4. Bodo, *The Way of St. Francis,* 165.
5. Margaret Ruth Miles, *Augustine on the Body* (Ann Arbor, Mich.: American Academy of Religion, 1979), 37.
6. Ibid.
7. Arthur A. Vogel, *Body Theology* (New York: Harper and Row, 1973), *ix.*
8. Ibid.
9. Charles Davis, *Body as Spirit: The Nature of Religious Feeling* (New York: Seabury Press, 1976), 37–38.
10. Sarano, *Meaning of the Body,* 180.
11. Ari L. Goldman, "Portrait of Religion in U.S. Holds Dozens of Surprises," *New York Times,* April 10, 1991, A–18.
12. *Daily Word* 129, no. 1 (1991): 10.

13. George Vecsey, "As They Look Past Their Riches, Athletes Are Turning to Religion," *New York Times,* April 29, 1991, A–21.
14. William A. Barry, S.J., *Finding God in All Things: A Companion to the Spiritual Exercises of St. Ignatius* (Notre Dame, Ind.: Ave Maria Press, 1991), 40.
15. Bodo, *The Way of St. Francis,* 21.
16. William Johnston, S.J., *Christian Zen* (New York: Harper and Row, 1973), 100.
17. Daniel Goleman, "Therapists See Religion as Aid Not Illusion," *New York Times,* September 10, 1991, C–1.
18. Vogel, *Body Theology,* 100.

Chapter 2: Prayer and Healing

1. Brother Roger, "Letter to Youth from Taizé," speech, spring 1992.
2. Randolph C. Byrd, "Positive Therapeutic Effects of Intercessary Prayer in a Coronary Care Unit Population," *Southern Medical Journal* 81, no. 7 (1988): 829.
3. Bruce Jancin, "Death Risk After Heart Surgery Rises for Patients with No Religious Beliefs," *Internal Medicine News* 26, no. 14 (July 15, 1993): 26.
4. Martin Millisin, "Spirituality and the Caregiver: Developing an Underutilized Facet of Care," *American Journal of Hospice Care* (March/April 1988): 37.
5. *Daily Word* 129, no. 2 (February 1991): 43.
6. Dorothy C. H. Ley and Inge B. Corless, *Spirituality and Hospice Care: Death Studies* (Chapel Hill, N.C.: Hemisphere Publishing Company, 1988), 105.
7. Ibid., 106.

Chapter 3: Some Frequent Signs of the Aging Process

1. Barbara Weinstein, "Geriatric Hearing Loss: Myths, Realities, Resources for Physicians," *Geriatrics* 44, no. 4 (1989): 46.
2. Steven R. Gambert and Krishan L. Gupta, "Preventive Care: What Is Its Worth in Geriatrics?" *Geriatics* 44, no. 8 (1989): 62.
3. Lewis Sudarsky, "Gait Disorders in the Elderly," *New England Journal of Medicine* 322, no. 20 (May 17, 1990): 1444.
4. Gary Gottlieb, "Sleep Disorders and their Management," *American Journal of Medicine* 88, suppl. 3A (May 2, 1990): 31S.
5. Patricia Prinz, Michael V. Vitiello, Murray A. Raskind, and Michael J. Thorpy, "Geriatrics: Sleep Disorders and Aging," *New England Journal of Medicine* 323, no. 8 (August 23, 1991): 524.

6. Eugene L. Coodley, "Coronary Artery Disease in the Elderly," *Postgraduate Medicine* 78, no. 2 (1990): 223.
7. W. F. Enos, R. H. Holmes, and J. Beyer, "Coronary Disease among United States Soldiers Killed in Action in Korea: Preliminary Report," *Journal of the American Medical Association* 152, no. 12 (July 18, 1953): 1090.
8. J. J. McNamara, M. A. Molet, J. F. Stremple, and R. T. Cutting, "Coronary Artery Disease in Combat Casualties in Vietnam," *Journal of the American Medical Association* 216, no. 7 (May 17, 1971): 1185–87.
9. Jonathan Fielding, "Smoking: Health Effects and Control," *New England Journal of Medicine* 313, no. 8 (1985): 491.

Chapter 4: Cultivating and Maintaining a Healthy Lifestyle

1. George H. Gallup, Jr., and Robert Bezilla, *The Religious Life of Young Americans* (Princeton, N.J.: George H. Gallup International Institute, 1992), 13.
2. George H. Gallup, Jr., and Robert Bezilla, *Religion in America, 1992–1993* (Princeton, N.J.: Princeton Religions Research Center, 1993), 55.
3. Richard Bach, *One* (New York: William Morrow, 1988), 48.
4. Laurence Freeman, O.S.B., "Commentary," *Living with Christ* 16, no. 2 (1992): 37.
5. Henri J. M. Nouwen, "Home," lecture, Dayspring Farm, Germantown, Md., October 28, 1992.
6. Winifred Gallegher, "Midlife Myths," *The Atlantic Monthly,* May 1993, 51–68.

Chapter 5: The Mystique of Remaining Young

1. Thomas Moore, *Care of the Soul* (New York: Harper Collins, 1992), 276.

Chapter 6: The Rapidly Aging Population

1. Edward G. LaKatta, Takashi Makinodan, and Paula S. Timaras, "The Aging Process," *Annals of Internal Medicine* 113 (1990): 455.
2. Sidney Katz, Lawrence G. Branch, Michael Branson, Joseph A. Papsidero, John Beck, and David S. Greer, "Active Life Expectancy," *New England Journal of Medicine* 297, no. 20 (1983): 1218.
3. John W. Rowe, "Clinical Research on Aging: Strategies and Directions," *New England Journal of Medicine* 297, no. 24 (1977): 1332.

4. Allen F. Shaughnessy, "Common Drug Interaction in the Elderly," *Emergency Medicine* (January 15, 1992): 21.
5. Rowe, "Clinical Research on Aging," 1336.
6. Charlotte D. Kain, Nancy Reilly, and Elaine D. Schultz, "The Older Adult," *Nursing Clinics of North America* 25, no. 4 (1990): 33.
7. Jean Vanier, "In the Face of the Poor," *The Word among Us* 10, no. 11 (1991): 54.
8. Rev. Bruce M. Webber, sermon given at Trinity Episcopal Church, Princeton, N.J., February 16, 1992.
9. Barry, *Finding God in All Things,* 138.
10. Steven E. Locke, Linda Kraus, Jane Leserman, and R. Michael Williams, "Life Changes, Stress, Psychiatric Symptoms, and Natural Killer Cell Activity," *Psychosomatic Medicine* 46 (September/ October 1984): 441.
11. Daniel Goleman, "Researchers Find That Optimism Helps the Body's Defense System," *New York Times,* April 20, 1989, Health section.

Chapter 7: Tobacco and Cardiovascular Disease

1. Fielding, "Smoking: Health Effects and Control," 491.
2. "Reducing Youth Access to Tobacco," *Journal of the American Medical Association* 226, no. 22 (December 11, 1991): 3186.
3. William F. Haynes, V. Krystulovic, and A. Loomis Bell, "Smoking Habit and Incidence of Respiratory Tract Infections in a Group of Adolescent Males," *American Review of Respiratory Diseases* 93 (1966): 730.
4. Gerald S. Berensen, Sasthanur R. Srinivason, Saundra MacD. Hunter, Theresa A. Nicklas, David S. Freedman, Charles L. Shear, and Larry S. Webber, "Risk Factors in Early Life as Predictors of Adult Heart Disease: The Bogalusa Heart Study," *American Journal of the Medical Sciences* 298, no. 3 (1989): 141–51.
5. Antonia C. Novello, "Report from the Surgeon General, U.S. Public Health Service; Tobacco Control," *Journal of the American Medical Association* 270, no. 7 (August 18, 1993): 806.
6. Phil Gunby, "Health Experts to Youth: Don't Give Tobacco a Start," *Journal of the American Medical Association* 271, no. 8 (February 23, 1994), 580.
7. Gideon Koren, Chrisoula Elipoulos, Julia Klein, My Khanh Phan, Brenda Knie, Mark Greenwald, and David Chitayat, "Hair Concentrations of Nicotine and Cotinine in Women and Their Newborn Infants," *Journal of the American Medical Association* 271, no. 8 (February 23, 1994): 621.

8. Harvey D. White, John T. Rivers, David B. Cross, Barbara Williams, and Robin Norris, "The Effect of Continued Smoking after Thrombolytic Therapy for Myocardial Infarction," *Cardiology Board Review* 8, no. 7 (1991): 42.
9. Fielding, "Smoking: Health Effects and Control," 491.
10. Ibid.
11. Kyle Steenland, "Passive Smoking and the Risk of Heart Disease," *Journal of the American Medical Association* 267, no. 1 (January 1992): 94.
12. Sheila West, "Does Smoke Get in Your Eyes?" *Journal of the American Medical Association* 268, no. 8 (August 26, 1992): 1025.

Chapter 8: Stress and Retirement

1. Raymond Bosse, Carolyn M. Aldwin, Michael R. Levinson, and Kathryn Workman-Daniels, "How Stressful Is Retirement? Findings from the Normative Aging Study," *Journal of Gerontology* 46, no. 1 (1991): 9.
2. Ibid., 12.
3. Hans Selye, *The Stress of Life,* rev. ed. (New York: McGraw-Hill, 1978), 413.
4. Carl Shusterman, "Retirement: The Last Day on the Job," *American Laundry Digest,* October 15, 1993, 16.
5. John W. James and Frank Cherry, *The Grief Recovery Handbook* (New York: Harper and Row, 1988), 133.
6. Robert S. Eliot, *Stress and the Major Cardiovascular Disorders* (Mount Kisco, N.Y.: Futura Publishing Co., 1979), 11.
7. Goleman, "Researchers Find That Optimism Helps the Body's Defense System," Health section.

Chapter 9: Exercise and the Aging Body Temple

1. Luba Vikhanski, "Exercise May Avert Diabetes," *Medical Tribune* 33, no. 12 (1992): 1.
2. Claudia Deutch, "Rewarding Employees for Wellness," *New York Times,* September 15, 1991, F–21.
3. Laurel A. Steinhaus, Robert E. Dustman, Robert O. Ruhling, Rita Y. Emmerson, Stephen C. Johnson, Donald E. Shearer, Richard W. Latin, John W. Shigeoka, and William H. Bonecat, "Aerobic Capacity of Older Adults: A Training Study," *Journal of Sports Medicine and Physical Fitness* 30, no. 2 (June 1990): 163, 169, 171.
4. Paul Rousseau, "Exercises in the Elderly," *Postgraduate Medicine* 85, no. 6 (1989): 116.

5. R. E. Frisch, "Lower Prevalence of Breast Cancer and Cancer of the Reproductive System among Former College Athletes Compared to Nonathletes," *British Journal of Cancer* 52 (1985): 885.

6. Roy J. Shephard, "The Scientific Basis of Exercise Prescribing for the Very Old," *Journal of the American Geriatric Society* 38, no. 1 (1990): 62.

7. Nancy E. Lane, Daniel A. Bloch, and James F. Fries, "Aging, Long-Distance Running, and the Development of Musculoskeletal Disability," *American Journal of Medicine* 82 (1987): 772.

8. Yukitoshi Aoyagi and Shigeru Katsuta, "The Relationship between the Starting Age of Training and Physical Fitness in Old Age," *Canadian Journal of Sports Science* 15, no. 1 (1990): 66.

9. Phil Whitten, "Just How Much Do We Decline with Age?" *Swim* 8, no. 4 (1992): 17, 20.

10. Steinhaus, Dustman, Ruhling, Emmerson, Johnson, Shearer, Latin, Shigeoka, Bonecat, "Aerobic Capacity of Older Adults," 163–71.

11. "Is It Possible to Age More Slowly?" Special Report, *U.S. News and World Report* 9, no. 7 (September 1991): 3.

12. David R. Hopkins, Betty Murrah, Werner W. K. Hoeger, and Colbert R. Rhodes, "The Effect of Low-Impact Aerobic Dance on the Functional Fitness of Elderly Women," *The Gerontologist* 30, no. 2 (1990): 189.

13. J. F. Nichols, "Efficacy of Heavy Resistance Training for Active Women over Sixty: Muscular Strength, Body Composition, and Program Adherence," *Journal of the American Geriatric Society* 41 (March 1993): 205.

14. "Is It Possible to Age More Slowly?" 3.

15. Paula P. Schnurr, Caroline O. Vaillant, George E. Vaillant, "Predicting Exercise in Late Midlife from Young Adult Personality Characteristics," *International Journal of Aging and Human Development* 30, no. 2 (1990): 153.

16. Theodore R. Bashore, J. M. Martiniere, P. C. Weiser, L. W. Green-span, and E. F. Heffley, "Preservation of Mental Processing Speed in Aerobically Fit Older Men," *Psychotherapy* 25 (1988): 433.

17. Ira Berkow, "The Old, the Dream, and Nolan," *New York Times,* May 3, 1991, Sports section.

18. Gerald Eskenazi, "Professor's Times Keep Falling, As Time Goes By," *New York Times,* May 27, 1991, 26.

19. Vic Sussman, "Muscle Bound," *U.S. News and World Report,* May 20, 1991, 85–87.

20. William Evans, "Muscle Bound," *U.S. News and World Report,* May 20, 1991, 87.
21. John Skow, "It's Coming Back to Me Now," *Time,* April 22, 1991, 80.

Chapter 10: The Handicapped Body Temple

1. Ruth Hamel, "Getting into the Game: New Opportunities for Athletes with Disabilities," *The Physician and Sportsmedicine* 20, no. 11 (1992): 124.
2. Freeman, "Commentary," *Living with Christ,* 73.
3. Bill Irwin with David McCasland, *Blind Courage* (Waco, Tex.: WRS Publishing, 1993), 98.

Chapter 11: Aging and Osteoporosis

1. Robert Marcus, "Understanding and Preventing Osteoporosis," *Hospital Practice* 24, no. 4 (April 15, 1989): 189.
2. Ibid., 215.
3. David R. Rudy, "Osteoporosis," *Postgraduate Medicine* 86, no. 2 (August 1989): 151.
4. Mona M. Shangold, "Exercise in the Menopausal Woman," *Obstetrics and Gynecology* 75, no. 4 (supplement) (April 1990): 56S.
5. Mehrsheed Sinaki, "Exercise and Osteoporosis," *Archives of Physical Medicine and Rehabilitation* 70 (March 1989): 220.
6. Frances Munnings, "Osteoporosis: What Is the Role of Exercise?" *The Physician and Sportsmedicine* 20, no. 6 (1992): 135.
7. Marcus, "Understanding and Preventing Osteoporosis," 215.
8. Munnings, "Osteoporosis: What Is the Role of Exercise?" 127.

Chapter 12: Nutrition and the Body Temple

1. Jerod M. Loeb, "Diet and Cancer: Where Do Matters Stand? Report of the Council on Scientific Affairs," *Archives of Internal Medicine* 153 (January 1993): 50.
2. P. J. Skerret, "Mighty Vitamins," *Medical World News* (January 1993): 24.
3. Gambert and Gupta, "Preventive Care," 63.
4. Ron Goor, Nancy Goor, and Katherine Boyd, *The Choose to Lose Diet* (Boston: Houghton Mifflin Company, 1990), 1.

Chapter 13: Psychological Aspects of Aging

1. Shannon Brownlee, "Alzheimer's: Is There Hope?" *U.S. News and World Report,* August 12, 1991, 40.
2. Ibid., 47.
3. Thomas Robischon, "Alzheimer Drugs in Development: Cautious Optimism," *Internal Medicine World Report* 7, no. 5 (March 1992): 12.
4. Ibid., 13.
5. Karen I. Bolla, Karen N. Lindgren, Cathy Bonaccorsy, and Margit L. Bleeker, "Memory Complaints in Older Adults, Fact or Fiction?" *Archives of Neurology* 48 (January 1991): 61.
6. Patricia A. Parmele and M. Powell Lawton, "The Relation of Pain to Depression among Institutionalized Aged," *Journal of Gerontology: Psychological Sciences* 26, no. 1 (1991): 21.
7. Theodore R. Bashore, "Age, Physical Fitness, and Mental Processing Speed," in *Annual Review of Gerontology and Geriatrics,* ed. M. Powell Lawton, vol. 9 (New York: Springer Publishing, 1990), 120–44.
8. R. E. Dustman, R. Y. Emmerson, R. O. Ruhling, D. E. Shearer, L. A. Steinhaus, S. C. Johnson, H. W. Bonecat, and J. W. Sigeoka, "Age and Fitness Effects on EEG, ERP's, Visual Sensitivity, and Cognition," *Neurobiology of Aging* 11 (1990): 193.
9. Robert G. Ruegg, Sidney Zisook, and Neil R. Swerdlow, "Depression in the Aged: An Overview," *Psychiatric Clinics of North America* 11, no. 1 (March 1988): 83.
10. Jane E. Brody, "Depression in the Elderly: Old Notions Hinder Help," *New York Times,* February 9, 1994, C–13.
11. Barbara Graham, "Group Therapy Is the Latest Weapon Against Disease," *Vogue,* September 1991, 398.
12. Laurence J. Robbins, "Effectively Managing Confusion in the Elderly," *Geriatric Consultant* 10, no. 4 (February 29, 1992): 23.

Chapter 14: Repairing the Body Temple

1. R. Greg Brown, "The Familial Atherosclerosis Treatment Study (FATS)," symposium, Baylor College of Medicine, Houston, Texas, winter 1991, 53.
2. Ibid.
3. John P. Kane, Mary J. Malloy, Thomas A. Ports, Nancy Phillips, James C. Diehl, and Richard J. Havel, "Regression of Coronary Atherosclerosis during Treatment of Familial Hypercholesterolemia with Combined Drug Regimens," *Journal of the American Medical Association* 264, no. 23 (December 19, 1990): 3007.

4. Lyle H. McCarty, "Catheter Clears Coronary Arteries," *Design News,* September 23, 1991, 88.
5. Thomas Robischon, "Who Should Receive Scarce Donor Hearts to Maximize Candidate Survival?" *Internal Medicine World Report* 7, no. 2 (January 15, 1992): 28.
6. Janice Hopkins Tanne, "Who Lives, Who Dies; Deciding Who Gets a Heart Transplant and Who Doesn't," *New York Magazine,* June 25, 1990, 33.
7. Robert Carlson, "Expanding the Heart Donor Pool," *Cardiology World News* 8, no. 1 (February 1992): 23.
8. Arlene B. Levine and T. Barry Levine, "Patient Evaluation for Cardiac Transplantation," *Progress in Cardiovascular Disease* 33, no. 4 (1991): 219.
9. Robert G. Clouse and Rodney Clapp, "A Little Victory over Death," *Christianity Today* 32, no. 5 (1988): 17.
10. Brother David Steindl-Rast, *A Listening Heart: The Art of Contemplative Living* (New York: Crossroad, 1989), 12.
11. Marion Noll, O.S.U., "Essay," *Living with Christ* 15, no. 4 (April 7, 1991): 47.
12. Andrea Kott, "Organ Procurement Programs in a State of Emergency," *Medical World News* (February 1992): 15–16.

Chapter 15: Genetic Engineering

1. John Pekkanen, "Genetics: Medicine's Amazing Leap," *Reader's Digest,* September 1991, 24.
2. John Bowersox, "Recombinant Molecules May Mean Improved Toxin Therapies," *Journal of the National Cancer Institute* 84, no. 19 (1992): 1466.
3. Spyros Andreopoulos, "Cancer Progress," *Stanford Observer* (September/October 1992): 1.
4. Eric Lander, lecture, Princeton University, spring 1992.
5. Leon Jaroff, *The New Genetics: The Human Genome Project and Its Impact on the Practice of Medicine* (Knoxville, Tenn.: Whittle Direct Books, 1991), 64.
6. Ibid., 65.
7. Pekkanen, "Genetics," 23.
8. "Activase," *The Physician's Desk Reference* (Montvale, N.J.: Medical Economics Company, 1992), 1047.
9. Pekkanen, "Genetics," 30.
10. Natalie Angier, "U.S. Clears Use of Gene Therapy against a Form of Lung Cancer," *New York Times,* September 16, 1992, A–20.
11. Pekkanen, "Genetics," 23.

Chapter 16: The End: Parting with the Body Temple

1. Kerry Dooley, "Area Woman Coordinates Organ Transplants in the State," *Princeton Packet,* December 17, 1991, 15–A.
2. Andrea Kott, "Commentary," *Medical World News* (February 1992): 15.

Summary

1. Natalie Goldberg, *Writing Down the Bones* (Boston: Shambhala Publications, 1986), 76.
2. Sarano, *The Meaning of the Body,* 189.

Bibliography

Articles and Essays

Andreopoulos, Spyros. "Cancer Progress." *Stanford Observer* (September–October 1992): 1.

Angier, Natalie. "U.S. Clears Use of Gene Therapy against a Form of Lung Cancer." *New York Times,* September 16, 1992, A–20.

Aoyagi, Yukitoshi, and Shigeru Katsuta. "The Relationship between the Starting Age of Training and Physical Fitness in Old Age." *Canadian Journal of Sports Science* 15, no. 1 (1990): 65–71.

Bashore, Theodore R. "Age, Physical Fitness, and Mental Processing Speed." In *Annual Review of Gerontology and Geriatrics,* edited by M. Powell Lawton, 120–44. Vol. 9. New York: Springer Publishing, 1990.

Bashore, Theodore R., J. M. Martiniere, P. C. Weiser, L. W. Greenspan, and E. F. Heffley. "Preservation of Mental Processing Speed in Aerobically Fit Older Men." *Psychotherapy* 25 (1988): 433–34.

Berensen, Gerald S., Sasthanur R. Srinivason, Saundra MacD. Hunter, Theresa A. Nicklas, David S. Freedman, Charles L. Shear, and Larry S. Webber. "Risk Factors in Early Life as Predictors of Adult Heart Disease: The Bogalusa Heart Study." *American Journal of the Medical Sciences* 298, no. 3 (1989): 141–51.

Berkow, Ira. "The Old, the Dream, and Nolan." *New York Times,* May 3, 1991.

Bolla, Karen I., Karen N. Lindgren, Cathy Bonaccorsy, and Margit L. Bleeker. "Memory Complaints in Older Adults, Fact or Fiction?" *Archives of Neurology* 48 (January 1991): 61–64.

Bosse, Raymond, Carolyn M. Aldwin, Michael R. Levinson, and Kathryn Workman-Daniels. "How Stressful Is Retirement? Findings from the Normative Aging Study." *Journal of Gerontology* 46, no. 1 (1991): 9–14.

Bowersox, John. "Recombinant Molecules May Mean Improved Toxin Therapies." *Journal of the National Cancer Institute* 84, no. 19 (1992): 1466–68.

Brody, Jane E. "Depression in the Elderly: Old Notions Hinder Help." *New York Times,* February 9, 1994, C–13.

Brownlee, Shannon. "Alzheimer's: Is There Hope?" *U.S. News and World Report,* August 12, 1991, 40–49.

Byrd, Randolph C. "Positive Therapeutic Effects of Intercessary Prayer in a Coronary Care Unit Population." *Southern Medical Journal* 81, no. 7 (1988): 826–29.

Carlson, Robert. "Expanding the Heart Donor Pool." *Cardiology World News* 8, no. 1 (February 1992): 23.

Clouse, Robert G. and Rodney Clapp. "A Little Victory over Death." *Christianity Today* 32, no. 5 (1988): 17–23.

Coodley, Eugene L. "Coronary Artery Disease in the Elderly." *Postgraduate Medicine* 78, no. 2 (1990): 223–27.

Deutch, Claudia. "Rewarding Employees for Wellness." *New York Times,* September 15, 1991, F–21.

Dooley, Kerry. "Area Woman Coordinates Organ Transplants in the State." *Princeton Packet,* December 17, 1991, 15–A.

Dustman, R. E., R. Y. Emmerson, R. O. Ruhling, D. E. Shearer, L. A. Steinhaus, S. C. Johnson, H. W. Bonecat, and J. W. Sigeoka. "Age and Fitness Effects on EEG, ERP's, Visual Sensitivity, and Cognition." *Neurobiology of Aging* 11 (1990): 193–200.

Enos, W. F., R. H. Holmes, and J. Beyer. "Coronary Disease among United States Soldiers Killed in Action in Korea: Preliminary Report." *Journal of the American Medical Association* 152, no. 12 (July 18, 1953): 1090–93.

Eskenazi, Gerald. "Professor's Times Keep Falling, As Time Goes By." *New York Times,* May 27, 1991, 26.

Evans, William. "Muscle Bound." *U.S. News and World Report,* May 20, 1991, 87.

Fielding, Jonathan. "Smoking: Health Effects and Control." *New England Journal of Medicine* 313, no. 8 (1985): 491–97.

Freeman, Laurence, O.S.B. "Commentary." *Living with Christ* 16, no. 2 (1992).

Frisch, R. E. "Lower Prevalence of Breast Cancer and Cancer of the Reproductive System among Former College Athletes Compared to Nonathletes." *British Journal of Cancer* 52 (1985): 885–91.

Gallegher, Winifred. "Midlife Myths." *The Atlantic Monthly,* May 1993, 51–68.

Gambert, Steven R., and Krishan L. Gupta. "Preventive Care: What Is Its Worth in Geriatrics?" *Geriatrics* 44, no. 8 (1989): 61–71.

Goldman, Ari L. "Portrait of Religion in U.S. Holds Dozens of Surprises." *New York Times,* April 10, 1991, A–18.

Goleman, Daniel. "Researchers Find That Optimism Helps the Body's Defense System." *New York Times,* April 20, 1989, Health section.

————. "Therapists See Religion as Aid Not Illusion." *New York Times.* September 10, 1991, C–1.

Gottlieb, Gary. "Sleep Disorders and Their Management." *American Journal of Medicine* 88, suppl. 3A (May 2, 1990): 3A–31S.

Graham, Barbara. "Group Therapy Is the Latest Weapon Against Disease." *Vogue,* September 1991.

Gunby, Phil. "Health Experts to Youth: Don't Give Tobacco a Start." *Journal of the American Medical Association* 271, no. 8 (February 23, 1994): 580.

Hamel, Ruth. "Getting into the Game: New Opportunities for Athletes with Disabilities." *The Physician and Sportsmedicine* 20, no. 11 (1992): 121–29.

Haynes, William F., V. Krystulovic, and A. Loomis Bell. "Smoking Habit and Incidence of Respiratory Tract Infections in a Group of Adolescent Males." *American Review of Respiratory Diseases* 93 (1966): 730–35.

Hopkins, David R., Betty Murrah, Werner W. K. Hoeger, and Colbert R. Rhodes. "The Effect of Low-Impact Aerobic Dance on the Functional Fitness of Elderly Women." *The Gerontologist* 30, no. 2 (1990): 189–92.

"Is It Possible to Age More Slowly?" Special report. *U.S. News and World Report* 9, no. 7 (September 1991): 3–6.

Jancin, Bruce. "Death Risk After Heart Surgery Rises for Patients with No Religious Beliefs." *Internal Medicine News* 26, no. 14 (July 15, 1993): 26.

Kain, Charlotte D., Nancy Reilly, Elaine D. Schultz. "The Older Adult." *Nursing Clinics of North America* 25, no. 4 (1990): 833–48.

Kane, John P., Mary J. Malloy, Thomas A. Ports, Nancy Phillips, James C. Diehl, and Richard J. Havel. "Regression of Coronary Atherosclerosis during Treatment of Familial Hypercholesterolemia with Combined Drug Regimens." *Journal of the American Medical Association* 264, no. 23 (December 19, 1990): 3007–12.

Katz, Sidney, Lawrence G. Branch, Michael Branson, Joseph A. Papsidero, John Beck, and David S. Greer. "Active Life Expectancy." *New England Journal of Medicine* 297, no. 20 (1983): 1218–23.

Koren, Gideon, Chrisoula Elipoulos, Julia Klein, My Khanh Phan, Brenda Knie, Mark Greenwald, and David Chitayat. "Hair Concentrations of Nicotine and Cotinine in Women and Their

Newborn Infants." *Journal of the American Medical Association* 271, no. 8 (February 23, 1994): 621–23.

Kott, Andrea. "Commentary." *Medical World News* (February 1992): 15.

———. "Organ Procurement Programs in a State of Emergency." *Medical World News* (February 1992): 15–16.

LaKatta, Edward G., Takashi Makinodan, and Paula S. Timaras. "The Aging Process." *Annals of Internal Medicine* 113, no. 6 (1990): 455–66.

Lane, Nancy E., Daniel A. Bloch, and James F. Fries. "Aging, Long-Distance Running, and the Development of Musculoskeletal Disability." *American Journal of Medicine* 82 (April 1987): 772–80.

Levine, Arlene B., and T. Barry Levine. "Patient Evaluation for Cardiac Transplantation." *Progress in Cardiovascular Disease* 33, no. 4 (1991): 219–28.

Locke, Steven E., Linda Kraus, Jane Leserman, and R. Michael Williams. "Life Changes, Stress, Psychiatric Symptoms, and Natural Killer Cell Activity." *Psychosomatic Medicine* 46 (September/October 1984).

Loeb, Jerod M. "Diet and Cancer: Where Do Matters Stand? Report of the Council on Scientific Affairs." *Archives of Internal Medicine* 153 (January 1993): 50–54.

Marcus, Robert. "Understanding and Preventing Osteoporosis." *Hospital Practice* 24, no. 4 (April 15, 1989): 189–218.

McCarty, Lyle H. "Catheter Clears Coronary Arteries." *Design News,* September 23, 1991, 88–92.

McNamara, J. J., M. A. Molet, J. F. Stremple, and R. T. Cutting. "Coronary Artery Disease in Combat Casualties in Vietnam." *Journal of the American Medical Association* 216, no. 7 (May 17, 1971): 1185–87.

Millisin, Martin. "Spirituality and the Caregiver: Developing an Underutilized Facet of Care." *American Journal of Hospice Care* (March/April 1988): 37–44.

Munnings, Frances. "Osteoporosis: What Is the Role of Exercise?" *The Physician and Sportsmedicine* 20, no. 6 (1992): 127–38.

Nichols, J. F. "Efficacy of Heavy Resistance Training for Active Women over Sixty: Muscular Strength, Body Composition, and Program Adherence." *Journal of the American Geriatric Society* 41 (March 1993): 205–10.

Noll, Marion, O.S.U. "Essay." *Living with Christ* 15, no. 4 (April 7, 1991): 47.

Parmele, Patricia A., and M. Powell Lawton. "The Relation of Pain to Depression among Institutionalized Aged." *Journal of Gerontology: Psychological Sciences* 26, no. 1 (1991): 15–21.

Pekkanen, John. "Genetics: Medicine's Amazing Leap." *Reader's Digest,* September 1991, 23–32.

Pierson, Paul. "The Easy Way." *Daily Word* 129, no. 1 (1991): 10.

Prinz, Patricia, Michael V. Vitiello, Murray A. Raskind, and Michael J. Thorpy. "Geriatrics: Sleep Disorders and Aging." *New England Journal of Medicine* 323, no. 8 (August 23, 1991): 524.

"Reducing Youth Access to Tobacco." *Journal of the American Medical Association* 226, no. 22 (December 11, 1991): 3186.

Robbins, Laurence J. "Effectively Managing Confusion in the Elderly." *Geriatric Consultant* 10, no. 4 (February 29, 1992): 23.

Robischon, Thomas. "Alzheimer Drugs in Development: Cautious Optimism." *Internal Medicine World Report* 7, no. 5 (March 1992): 12–13.

———. "Who Should Receive Scarce Donor Hearts to Maximize Candidate Survival?" *Internal Medicine World Report* 7, no. 2 (January 15, 1992): 28.

Rousseau, Paul. "Exercises in the Elderly." *Postgraduate Medicine* 85, no. 6 (1989): 113–16.

Rowe, John. "Clinical Research on Aging: Strategies and Directions." *New England Journal of Medicine* 297, no. 24 (1977): 1332–36.

Rudy, David R. "Osteoporosis." *Postgraduate Medicine* 86, no. 2 (August 1989): 151–58.

Ruegg, Robert G., Sidney Zisook, and Neil R. Swerdlow. "Depression in the Aged: An Overview." *Psychiatric Clinics of North America* 11, no. 1 (March 1988): 83–99.

Schnurr, Paula P., Caroline O. Vaillant, George E. Vaillant. "Predicting Exercise in Late Midlife from Young Adult Personality Characteristics." *International Journal of Aging and Human Development* 30, no. 2 (1990): 153–60.

Shangold, Mona M. "Exercise in the Menopausal Woman." *Obstetrics and Gynecology* 75, no. 4. Supplement (April 1990): 53S–58S.

Shaughnessy, Allen F. "Common Drug Interaction in the Elderly." *Emergency Medicine* (January 15, 1992): 21–32.

Shephard, Roy J. "The Scientific Basis of Exercise Prescribing for the Very Old." *Journal of the American Geriatric Society* 38, no. 1 (1990): 62–70.

Shusterman, Carl. "Retirement: The Last Day on the Job." *American Laundry Digest,* October 15, 1993, 16–18.

Sinaki, Mehrsheed. "Exercise and Osteoporosis." *Archives of Physical Medicine and Rehabilitation* 70 (March 1989): 220–29.

Skerret, P. J. "Mighty Vitamins." *Medical World News* (January 1993): 24–32.

Skow, John. "It's Coming Back to Me Now." *Time,* April 22, 1991, 78–80.

Steenland, Kyle. "Passive Smoking and the Risk of Heart Disease." *Journal of the American Medical Association* 267, no. 1 (January 1992): 94–99.

Steinhaus, Laurel A., Robert E. Dustman, Robert O. Ruhling, Rita Y. Emmerson, Stephen C. Johnson, Donald E. Shearer, Richard W. Latin, John W. Shigeoka, and William H. Bonecat. "Aerobic Capacity of Older Adults: A Training Study." *Journal of Sports Medicine and Physical Fitness* 30, no. 2 (June 1990): 163–71.

Sudarsky, Lewis. "Gait Disorders in the Elderly." *New England Journal of Medicine* 322, no. 20 (May 17, 1990): 1441–45.

Sussman, Vic. "Muscle Bound." *U.S. News and World Report,* May 20, 1991, 85–87.

Tanne, Janice Hopkins. "Who Lives, Who Dies; Deciding Who Gets a Heart Transplant and Who Doesn't." *New York Magazine,* June 25, 1990, 28–38.

Vanier, Jean. "In the Face of the Poor." *The Word among Us* 10, no. 11 (1991): 54.

Vecsey, George. "As They Look Past their Riches, Athletes Are Turning to Religion." *New York Times,* April 29, 1991, A–21.

Vikhanski, Luba. "Exercise May Avert Diabetes." *Medical Tribune* 33, no. 12 (1992): 1.

Weinstein, Barbara. "Geriatric Hearing Loss: Myths, Realities, Resources for Physicians." *Geriatrics* 44, no. 4 (1989): 42–58.

West, Sheila. "Does Smoke Get in Your Eyes?" *Journal of the American Medical Association* 268, no. 8 (1992): 1025–26.

White, Harvey D., John T. Rivers, David B. Cross, Barbara Williams, and Robin Norris. "The Effect of Continued Smoking after Thrombolytic Therapy for Myocardial Infarction." *Cardiology Board Review* 8, no. 7 (1991): 42–52.

Whitten, Phil. "Just How Much Do We Decline with Age?" *Swim* 8, no. 4 (1992): 17–20.

Books

Ader, Robert, David L. Felten, and Nicholas Cohen. *Psychoneuroimmunology.* 2nd ed. San Diego: Academic Press, 1991.

Bach, Richard. *One.* New York: William Morrow, 1988.

Barry, William A., S.J. *Finding God in All Things: A Companion to the Spiritual Exercises of St. Ignatius.* Notre Dame, Ind.: Ave Maria Press, 1991.

Bodo, Murray, O.F.M. *The Way of St. Francis*. New York: Image Books/Doubleday, 1984.

Brother Roger of Taizé. *Parable of Community*. Oxford: A. R. Mowbury and Co., 1984.

Davis, Charles. *Body as Spirit: The Nature of Religious Feeling*. New York: Seabury Press, 1976.

Eliot, Robert S. *Stress and the Major Cardiovascular Disorders*. Mount Kisco, N.Y.: Futura Publishing Co., 1979.

Gallup, George H., Jr., and Robert Bezilla. *Religion in America, 1922–1993*. Princeton, N.J.: Princeton Religions Resource Center, 1993.

———. *The Religious Life of Young Americans*. Princeton, N.J.: George H. Gallup International Institute, 1992.

Goldberg, Natalie. *Writing Down the Bones*. Boston: Shambhala Publications, 1986.

Goor, Ron, Nancy Goor, and Katherine Boyd. *The Choose to Lose Diet*. Boston: Houghton Mifflin Company, 1990.

Haynes, William F. *A Physician's Witness to the Power of Shared Prayer*. Chicago: Loyola University Press, 1990.

Irwin, Bill, with David McCasland. *Blind Courage*. Waco, Tex.: WRS Publishing, 1993.

James, John W., and Frank Cherry. *The Grief Recovery Handbook*. New York: Harper and Row, 1988.

Jaroff, Leon. *The New Genetics: The Human Genome Project and Its Impact on the Practice of Medicine*. Knoxville, Tenn.: Whittle Direct Books, 1991.

Johnston, William, S.J. *Christian Zen*. New York: Harper and Row, 1973.

Ley, Dorothy C. H., and Inge B. Corless. *Spirituality and Hospice Care: Death Studies*. Chapel Hill, N.C.: Hemisphere Publishing Company, 1988.

Miles, Margaret Ruth. *Augustine on the Body*. Ann Arbor, Mich.: American Academy of Religion, 1979.

Moore, Thomas. *Care of the Soul*. New York: Harper Collins, 1992.

Nouwen, Henri J. M. *Show Me the Way*. New York: Crossroad, 1992.

Reuben, David, Thomas T. Yoshikawa, and Richard Besdine, eds. *Geriatrics Review: A Core Curriculum in Geriatric Medicine*. New York: American Geriatrics Society, 1993–94.

Sarano, Jacques. *The Meaning of the Body*. Trans. James H. Farley. Philadelphia: Westminster Press, 1966.

Selye, Hans. *The Stress of Life*. Rev. ed. New York: McGraw-Hill, 1978.

Shlemon, Barbara. *Healing the Hidden Self*. Notre Dame, Ind.: Ave Maria Press, 1982.

Steindl-Rast, Brother David. *A Listening Heart: The Art of Contemplative Living*. New York: Crossroad, 1989.

Vogel, Arthur A. *Body Theology*. New York: Harper and Row, 1973.

Index